LEA WITH TRADITIONAL PROJECTS

A CLASSIC PRACTICAL MANUAL FOR TECHNIQUE, TOOLING, EQUIPMENT, AND PLANS FOR HANDCRAFTED ITEMS

BY **PAUL N. HASLUCK**

ORIGINALLY PUBLISHED IN 1904

LEGACY EDITION

HASLUCK'S TRADITIONAL SKILLS LIBRARY
BOOK 3

Doublebit Press
Eugene, OR

Doublebit Press is an imprint of Eagle Nest Press
www.doublebitpress.com | Eugene, OR, USA

Original content under the public domain. Originally published in 1904 by Paul N. Hasluck under the title <u>LEATHER WORKING</u>.

This title, along with other Doublebit Press books including the Hasluck's Traditional Skills Library, are available at a volume discount for youth groups, outdoors clubs, or reading groups.

Doublebit Press Legacy Edition ISBNs
Hardcover: 978-1-64389-055-5
Paperback: 978-1-64389-056-2

First Doublebit Press Legacy Edition Printing, 2019

Printed in the United States of America
when purchased at retail in the USA

INTRODUCTION
To The Doublebit Press Legacy Edition

The old experts of artisanal trades, country and homestead knowledge, and the woods and mountains taught timeless principles and skills for centuries. Through their timeless books, the old experts offered rich descriptions of how the world works and encouraged learning through personal experiences *by doing*. Over the last 125 years, manufacturing, farming, and construction have substantially changed. Of course, many things have gotten simpler as equipment and technology have improved. In addition, some activities of pre-digital times are now no longer in vogue, or are even outright considered inappropriate or illegal. However, despite many of the positive changes in manufacturing and crafting methods that have occurred over the years, *there are many other skills and much knowledge that have been forgotten.*

By publishing *The Hasluck Traditional Skills Library*, it is our goal at Doublebit Press to do what we can to preserve and share the works from forgotten teachers that form the cornerstone of the history of the American artisans and traditional crafts. Through remastered reprint editions of timeless classics, perhaps we can regain some of this lost knowledge for future generations.

This book is an important contribution traditional handcraft and country skills literature and has important historical and collector value toward preserving the American handcraft and outdoors tradition. The knowledge it holds is an invaluable reference for practicing skills and hand craft methods. Its chapters thoroughly discuss some of the essential building blocks of knowledge that are fundamental but may have been forgotten as equipment gets fancier and technology gets smarter. In short, this book was chosen for Legacy Edition printing because much of the basic skills and knowledge it contains has been forgotten or put to the wayside in trade for more modern conveniences and methods.

With technology playing a major role in everyday life, sometimes we need to take a step back in time to find those basic building blocks used for gaining mastery – the things that we have luckily not completely lost and has been recorded in books over the last two centuries. These skills aren't forgotten, they've just been shelved. *It's time to unshelve them once again and reclaim the lost knowledge of self-sufficiency.*

Based on this commitment to preserving our outdoors and handcraft artisanal heritage, we have taken great pride in publishing this book as a complete original work. We hope it is worthy of both study and collection by outdoors folk in the modern era of outdoors and traditional skills life.

Unlike many other photocopy reproductions of classic books that are common on the market, this Legacy Edition does not simply place poor photography of old texts on our pages and use error-prone optical scanning or computer-generated text. We want our work to speak for itself, and reflect the quality demanded by our customers who spend their hard-earned money. With this in mind, each Legacy Edition book that has been chosen for publication is carefully remastered from original print books, *with the Doublebit Legacy Edition printed and laid out in the exact way that it was presented at its original publication.* We provide a beautiful, memorable experience that is as true to the original text as best as possible, but with the aid of modern technology to make as beautiful a reading experience as possible for books that can be over a century old.

Because of its age and because it is presented in its original form, the book may contain misspellings, inking errors from print plates, and other printing blemishes that were common for the age. However, these are exactly the things that we feel give the book its character, which we preserved in this Legacy Edition. During digitization, we ensured that each illustration in the text was clean and sharp with the least amount of loss from being copied and digitized as possible. Full-page plate illustrations are presented as they were found, often including the extra blank page that was often behind a plate. For the covers, we use the original cover design to give the book its original feel. We are sure you'll appreciate the fine touches and attention to detail that your Legacy Edition has to offer.

For traditional handcrafters and classic artisanal enthusiasts who demand the best from their equipment, this Doublebit Press Legacy Edition reprint was made with you in mind. Both important and minor details have equally both been accounted for by our publishing staff, down to the cover, font, layout, and images. It is the goal of Doublebit Legacy Edition series to be worthy of collection in any outdoorsperson's library and that can be passed to future generations.

Every book selected to be in this series offers unique views and instruction on important skills, advice, tips, tidbits, anecdotes, stories, and experiences that will enrichen the repertoire of any person who enjoys escaping a bit from today's modern technology-based, cookie-cutter, and highly industrialized skills. Instead, folks seeking to make things with their hands like the old days may find great value from these resurrected instructional manuals from the past. These books were not simply written to be shelved in a library – they contain our history and forgotten methods to make things with real character and energy with a *human* component.

Therefore, to learn the most basic building blocks of a craft leads to mastery of all its aspects. We hope this book helps you along this path with its rich descriptions and illustrations!

About Hasluck's Traditional Skills Library

Paul N. Hasluck was a prominent author on artisan skills and traditional handcrafts toward the end of the 19th Century. He was the editor of the magazine *Work*, which was a popular handcraft, shop skills, and artisanal craft magazine of the day. His broad expertise in making things with your hands led him to write or edit over 30 volumes on specific handcrafts, arts, and mechanics, with each manual containing invaluable information related to each craft.

Hasluck had a great eye for collecting the info that beginners and experts alike needed to perfect their craft. His volumes were loaded with helpful diagrams, tables, and illustrations that are useful even by today's digital standards. In short, Hasluck's instructional manuals were the *go-to instructional library* if someone wanted to learn a particular skill. Used by the U.S. military, the Boy and Girl Scouts, and countless folks at farms, public libraries, and homes across the world, Hasluck's instructional manuals were the perfect "handy book" for learning.

This Doublebit Press Legacy Edition republishes this tradition of handcrafted quality and artisanal work. We hope that this deluxe printed edition of this work will help you gain mastery in your craft, as it is presented in the exact form that it was originally published. Even today, the knowledge contained within its pages are timeless and have much to teach!

Finally, as art, Hasluck's manuals contain beautiful illustrations and line art that are a sign of simpler, yet authentic times when quality mattered and craftsmanship was king. This collectible volume makes a great addition to the bookshelf of any handcrafter, maker, artisan, farmer, homesteader, or outdoors enthusiast!

LEATHER WORKING

WITH NUMEROUS ENGRAVINGS AND DIAGRAMS

EDITED BY

PAUL N. HASLUCK

EDITOR OF "WORK" AND "BUILDING WORLD,"
AUTHOR OF "HANDYBOOKS FOR HANDICRAFTS," ETC. ETC.

PREFACE.

THIS Handbook contains, in a form convenient for everyday use, a comprehensive digest of the information on Leather Working, scattered over more than twenty thousand columns of WORK—one of the weekly journals it is my fortune to edit—and supplies concise information on the details of the subjects on which it treats.

In preparing for publication in book form the mass of relevant matter contained in the volumes of WORK, much had to be arranged anew, altered, and largely re-written. From these causes the contributions of many are so blended that the writings of individuals cannot be distinguished for acknowledgment.

Readers who may desire additional information respecting special details of the matters dealt with in this Handbook, or instructions on kindred subjects, should address a question to WORK, so that it may be answered in the columns of that journal.

P. N. HASLUCK.

La Belle Sauvage, London.
   May, 1904.

CONTENTS.

LIST OF ILLUSTRATIONS.

LEATHER WORKING.

CHAPTER I

QUALITIES AND VARIETIES OF LEATHER.

THIS handbook will describe how to make a large number of useful articles in leather. Naturally, some mention of tools must come first, but it is not thought necessary to give space to their description here, as they have already been dealt with so fully and illustrated so clearly in companion volumes, " Boot Making and Mending," and " Harness Making." They will be indicated sufficiently in later chapters as the need for their use arises. This chapter will discuss leather, its qualities and varieties.

Commercial skins are classified in Watt's " Art of Leather Manufacture " under three heads, namely : 1. Hides—or the skins of the large and full-grown animals, as the ox, cow, buffalo, horse, and hippopotamus ; 2. Kips—or the skins of the younger animals of the same class ; and 3. Skins—as those of the smaller animals, such as the calf, sheep, goat, deer, etc. The skins most extensively used in leather manufacture are those· of the ox, cow, horse, calf, sheep, goat, kid, pig, deer, seal, and kips, but recently the skins of crocodiles, alligators, and serpents have been employed for making certain kinds of fancy leather.

Particulars of the many varieties of leather may now be given.

Patent Calf.—In making this leather, the skin, having received its preliminary preparation, is stretched upon a smooth board, and every particle of grease extracted from it with fuller's-earth and water. It is then given four coats of varnish containing drying oil, vegetable black, and Prussian blue. As each coat is applied, the leather is stoved and afterwards polished with powdered pumice-stone. The final coat has an addition of darker Prussian blue, and sometimes a little copal or amber varnish. The stove heat varies from 120° to 180° F., according to the leather under treatment.

Waxed Calf.—After depilation and tanning, the skin has to pass through a variety of processes, namely soaking, fleshing and skiving, graining, finishing, stretching, stuffing, compo-ing, drying, whitening, blacking, sizing, polishing, etc. This will give some idea of the amount of handling a calf-skin goes through before it is converted to leather. French calf skins, especially "females," are the best, and softest in wear, although those of English production are, in some cases, very fine ; the latter, not being so soft, are more suitable for stronger and heavier work than French.

Memel Calf.—With few exceptions this is treated in the same way as waxed calf. In some cases the whole skin is treated ; but in a great many instances it is only the shoulders, or perhaps the necks, that are made into memel. It should be well tanned. The compo-ing is done on the grain side, and the stuffing on the flesh side, and not so much of either is needed as for wax calf. It is grained with a roller according to the sort of grain required, whether pebble, long, etc. After oiling, sizing, and drying, the graining is finished, the leather is finely oiled, and is then ready for use.

Russet Calf is used either dry or with a little oil dressing ; in the former case it is very pale, the oil making it a little darker. Horse and other animal belly rounding is now often dressed in a like manner.

Its preparation is similar in some respects to that of other dry-dressed leathers, and, among other processes, it passes through a solution of borax, weak sulphuric acid, and a warm bath of Sicily sumach and alum, which forms a mordant when further dyeing is needed.

Tan Calf has been produced to imitate Russia leather at less cost, and there now is a greater quantity used for the best class of work than of real Russia. Each season brings its varied and improved shades. The calf skin is such a ready recipient of dyes, that by manipulating with various mordants the expert leather dyer can produce some very delicate tints.

Ooze Calf is a very soft leather in wear, and most durable if kept well cleaned. It has a nice pebble grain, which generally forms the face. The flesh side is a velvet pile, and when first produced was considered the right side, and it was so made up and advertised as "velvet calf." But the grain is the side now generally preferred.

Calf Kid is a most useful leather made by tawing, not tanning. It has to pass through the following routine: Soaking, cleaning, liming, unhairing, fleshing, paring, scudding, drenching, alum and salt dressing, drying, seasoning, staking, shaving, egging, dyeing, and finishing. The difference between tanning and tawing is briefly this—When tanned, the greatest component part of a skin, namely gelatine, is, by the action of tannic acid, formed into leather, of which these two ingredients are the chief factors. The acid arrests decomposition, and the two ingredients cannot return to their former state; whereas, in tawing, alum, salt, and gelatine form the leather, and although the two former prevent decomposition of the gelatine, each ingredient can be brought back to its original state.

Glacé or French Kid is a very delicate and fine surfaced leather. It is subjected to a process of tawing

which imparts to it great suppleness. It is dyed
upon the grain side, except when bath dyed, which
is rarely the case, and is then glazed and polished.

Glove Kid is made into leather by tawing in the
same way as calf kid, but its character and uses are
quite different.

Cordovan is made in many places other than its
supposed place of origin—Cordova. It is tanned
and curried on the grain side, and passes through
some special processes, such as a bran bath and a
fig bath. It is made a good deal from horse, goat,
and even dog skin. An inferior leather, much like
it, called "grain," is used a good deal for cheaper
work, and a much newer production, called "satin-
hide," is a similar leather, but possesses a smoother
face. Cordovan stands easily first for durability,
satin-hide being next.

Morocco, Levant, is a beautifully grained and
tanned goat-skin, dyed on the grain side, and
finished with a bright pebble grain. A cheaper and
somewhat greasy kind is not nearly so good-looking
or durable in wear as the dry-dressed morocco
levant, which has a beautiful soft brightness. Skins
are produced in imitation of moroccos of various
colours. These are called roans, and are made from
sheep-skins, as "Cream Roans."

Brown Levant Morocco is the same as morocco
levant, except that it is made from younger and
smaller skins, and is more finely grained.

Long-grain Morocco is, like the two last-named,
made from the skin of goats, but has a long grain
running across the skin. These leathers are tanned
with sumach, provided by leaves and twigs. The
better kinds are the Strasbourg moroccos.

White Sheep is a tawed leather, and forms a very
soft material. Among the many processes it undergoes is the application of paste composed of flour
and yolks of eggs, in addition to the alum bath
which it has previously received.

Cream Roan is made generally from good (medium weight) sheep-skins, sumach tanned, and is similar in structure to morocco, though, like all sheep-skin, it is less durable.

Brown Persian is obtained as a rule from Cape sheep. It make a fine, soft, tough leather ; when dyed it resembles morocco, but is left with a smooth grain.

Skivers, Brown, etc.—This is the grain of sheep-skin split by machinery (the flesh side being prepared for chamois or wash-leather). In appearance it is much like brown persian, except that it is extremely thin. This is really bookbinders' skiver, and is used for covering fancy articles.

Cowhide Patent, or enamel hide, is made from the hide of the cow. The process of enamelling is the same as that for patent calf, though in this instance the enamelling is done upon the grain side after the grain has been printed or otherwise prepared. It is now produced with a smaller grain than in former years, when it had a longer grain like the leather now used for bags, etc. It is now known more by the name Diamond hide.

Black Grain (Cow) Hide.—This is treated somewhat as wax calf, but the dyeing is done on the grain side, and as much stuffing is put in as it will possibly hold.

Brown Cowhide is made into leather by some of the preceding methods ; it is worked in the same way as black grain cowhide, but it is very slightly stuffed in cases where the natural colour is not needed and dyeing has to be resorted to.

Porpoise-hide is tanned and very greasily dressed, and makes a very soft and waterproof leather. It is expensive, but is exceedingly durable.

Crup or Horse is taken generally from the butt of the horseskin. It is practically the middle part of the skin that is dressed for this leather, as the grain and a good quantity of flesh are taken off.

When good it wears well and is waterproof, and polishes more easily and better than calf. Its uses are the same as those of waxed calf.

Pigskin generally is dressed brown. It is a tanned leather, light in weight, porous, very durable, and soft and cool to wear.

Russia Leather is one of the best of brown leathers. According to Andrew Ure the process of dressing this leather is as follows: It is freed from hair, rinsed, fulled for a longer or shorter time according to the nature of the skin, and fermented in a proper steep (for a week at least) after a hot-water washing ; it is then worked on the beam after soaking for forty-eight hours in a bath containing a fermented paste of rye flour ; it is rinsed for fifteen days, then worked in the river, and subjected to the stringent juices of willow bark, etc. After a deal of working in this, it is set to dry and curried with empyreumatic oil of the bark of birch tree. To this substance the Russia leather owes its peculiarities. If the oil passes through it stains the grain side. The red colour is supposed to be from sandalwood or basil wood.

Kangaroo.—The skin of the kangaroo, when properly tanned, does not crack. It is one of the softest and prettiest leathers, and has been improved largely in recent years.

Buckskin.—To prepare this leather for use, the whole of the grain is cut away and oil is hammered into it, any excess of oil being removed afterwards. A vast amount of working is necessary to give it suppleness. Doe is similar, but not so good.

Brown Glacé Kid.—This and the two following are believed to be produced by chrome tanning. Brown glacé kid is an American production, and seems to vary much as regards retaining its colour in wear according to the shade given it, the bright browns lasting well, while the dull or subdued tints sometimes change under the influence of cream dressings.

Box Calf.—The grain side is the face of this leather. It is somewhat like firm ooze calf, only black, but resists moisture better. Many leathers are being made of this and a similar—green calf, for instance; also iron calf or kid, which is much like calf kid, but, from being dressed to resemble kid, is very useful, and an extremely strong leather.

Willow Calf is similar to box calf, but it is of a brown colour. It is made in good colours and retains them longer, perhaps, than any other sort of

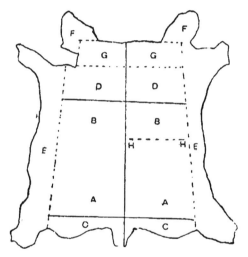

Fig. 1.—Method of Cutting up Hide.

brown leather, and is easy to clean and repolish. It is used for all purposes for which box calf is employed.

Foreign Butt (Bend) and Belly.—These, for the most part, are similar to the English butt, except that the processes of manufacture are different.

Basil is made by tanning the large and stouter kinds of sheepskins with oak and larch bark. This leather is generally used in the best class shoe trade only for pump inner-soles.

Welting is generally made from English shoul-

ders. These are converted into welting by being
stuffed well with grease. They are used for the
welts of hand-sewn boots and shoes.

It is now necessary to give a description of the
different parts of a hide of leather. Fig. 1 gives a
diagram of a hide, fully showing the various parts.
A A are the best parts of the butt; B B, top end;
C C, edge, or hitch pieces. The whole of above,
combined, are commercially called butt ends, while
with D D (the first cut) the whole would be a butt;
E E, part known as bellies; F F, odd pieces, with
others, are flanks, shanks, cheeks, and faces; G G,
shoulders; A B C D and G, folded at H H, are sides and
bends.

CHAPTER II.

In making a gross (144 pairs) of common garters ½ in. or ⅝ in. wide, the following tools will be required:—One hollow-ground knife ; one plain knife, not hollow-ground ; a punch (see p. 15 of " Harness Making "), with nipples from ¹⁄₁₆ in. to ⅛ in. in diameter ; a pair or two of pliers ; a screw-crease or two (see p. 19 of " Harness Making ") ; and a marking board of dry mahogany or any hard wood ½ in. to 1 in. thick, about 3 ft. long by 9 in. wide.

For the cutting board, use a piece of planed deal or pine free from knots ; mark from the end along one edge distances of 12½ in., 13½ in., 14½ in., and 15½ in. A hardwood measuring-off stick about 2 in. wide, 2 ft. long, and ½ in. thick should have the following lengths marked—12 in., 13 in., 14 in., and 15 in. An emery stick about 1 in. square, of any length, with emery paper glued round, a few wire nails 1½ in. long, and some leather and buckles, will be wanted. Glue a leather shaving on the back of each knife blade to 2 in. from the point, as a protection for the fingers gripping the blade when cutting the leather, which should be from ¹⁄₁₂ in. to ⅛ in. thick.

Begin to make the garters by placing the leather on the cutting board, and with the hollow-ground knife cut an edge of the leather straight. Then cut them out, using the thumbnail as a guide. An easy way is to set a pair of compasses or points to the required width of the strap (bare ⅝ in.), to cut an edge of the leather straight, and to run the points down the leather, which can then be cut to the mark made. Do not cut any shorter than the

B

$12\frac{1}{2}$-in. mark on the cutting board, and always examine the leather to see that there will not be much waste. Then point the lengths as in Fig. 2 with the other knife.

To mark the straps on the board, use the screw-crease set to $\frac{1}{12}$ in. The marking does not show up if not near the edge. Heat the point of the screw-crease in the gas or fire; when it is at the proper heat it will move easily along the strap, leaving a bright glossy mark if a little force is exerted. The top of the strap is not marked. A small can containing water in which to dip the crease when too hot should be at hand. In heating by gas, mount on the pipe a tin can about $1\frac{1}{2}$ in. in diameter. If the outside diameter of the gaspipe is $\frac{1}{2}$ in., cut down from the top with a pair of scissors two nicks about 1 in. long on opposite sides of the can; then bend up the tin, push the can on the gaspipe, bend the strips down, and tie them securely with band or wire. The screw-crease, when being heated, rests on the bottom of the can. Of course, a small gas stove will do as well, and probably better.

Now punch a hole A (Fig. 2) for the tongue of the buckle in each strap about $\frac{3}{4}$ in. from the top, and on the centre line; three or four straps can be punched at a time. Then cut the bits. In Fig. 3 two kinds are illustrated; A makes a better job, but is more difficult to cut than B. The edges can be marked to improve the appearance.

To buckle the garters, press the tongue of a buckle open and thread a strap through, putting the tongue in the hole A (Fig. 2) and bending back the $\frac{3}{4}$ in. threaded through, as in Fig. 4. Hold the garter in the left hand, pressing down the $\frac{3}{4}$-in. length with the thumbnail, and put one edge of a bit just under the thumbnail, holding it firm. Then with a punch in the right hand make a hole through the bit, the $\frac{1}{2}$-in. length, and the front of the strap. Lap the point of the bit from the back round the

front, and thread it through the hole. Put the
buckle on a nail in the table and pull the bit A
(Fig. 4) with the pliers. Cut the bit, leaving it
about ⅛ in. long. Then fasten the measuring off
board to the table with a couple of springs, and
measure the garters one at a time, putting together
those measuring to 12½ in. long, then those measur-

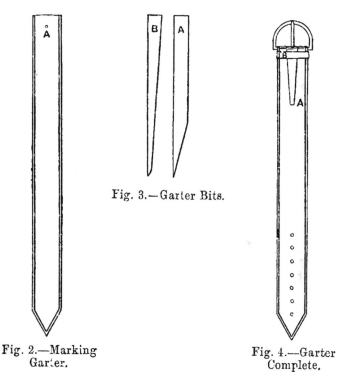

Fig. 3.—Garter Bits.

Fig. 2.—Marking
Garter.

Fig. 4.—Garter
Complete.

ing to 13½ in., those measuring to 14½ in., and those
measuring to 15½ in., calling them 12s, 13s, 14s, and
15s.

For pairing, take a measured pile, then place two
of the garters side by side and see whether they are
of equal widths, and whether one is, say, ¼ in. to
½ in. longer than the other. Then push the point
of the longer garter through the bit marked B

(Fig. 4) of the other ; pull it through, when the points of the two garters should come fair. Thus the top garter of a pair is slightly the longer, the width of the bit on the shorter garter making the difference.

Next punch the garters down the leg, doing a pair together at first, until with practice two pairs can be done at once. Make six holes in the 12s and 13s, and seven in the 14s and 15s, the rule being half as many holes as the strap is inches long. The holes should just let the buckle tongues pass through.

Packing may be done by the round way or the length way. By the first method, place three of the 12s, one at a time, on the table with the flesh side facing the worker ; then pack three 13s as before, putting them at the back of the 12s, then pick three 14s, putting them at the back of the 13s, then three 15s at the back of the 14s. Twist the straps round, and it will be seen that the longer ones wrap round the shorter garters. Then tie the ends with band. For the length way, half a dozen garters are placed lengthwise one way and the other half dozen the other way, the shorter garters being packed in the middle. Three bands are tied across, one at each of the ends and one at the middle. The garters are packed in dozens and in half or whole grosses.

Leg straps are like garters, but generally have a roller buckle, and are 18 in. to 21 in. long ; rather stronger leather is used, and the straps are $\frac{5}{8}$ in. wide.

Skate straps are generally $\frac{5}{8}$ in. wide, and from 18 in. to 36 in. long, and can be made as above described, but for a stronger job the buckle tongue hole should be about 1 in. from the top. Then the point of the bit can be threaded through a hole punched on the centre line of the strap. They can also be made with double buckles, one part serving as the bit. They are either riveted or sewn.

Skate straps are also made with roller buckles. The strap is prepared as described, except that the bit is cut to Fig. 5 to go round the strap and meet at the back ; then punch a hole in the centre of each end, and with twine thread through both holes, pull the ends together, and tie. Then press the bits so that the knots are at the back, and slip one on each strap to the buckle. A rivet is put in just below the bit and goes through the portion which is lapped over ; or the pieces can be sewn by hand or machine.

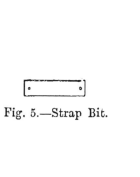

Fig. 5.—Strap Bit.

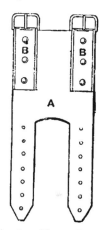

Fig. 6.—Skate Strap.

In another form of skate strap (shown in Fig. 6), the part A is set out with a zinc template, and the two small garters B, which are riveted on, are about 3 in. long. The strap for these should be 6 in. long, and the hole for the buckle tongue should be punched in the centre, so that when they are fastened the rivets go through the back part as well as through the front. Sometimes this skate strap is curved a little, one strap being curved one way for one foot, and the other the other way. They are from 12 in. to 20 in. long and from 2 in. to 3 in. broad, and hold the front part of the skate, a strap from 18 in. to 21 in. holding the back part.

Pareel straps, 30 in. to 40 in. long, are made as described above, and are threaded through a nickel-plated, brass, or leather handle.

Dog-leads are handier for general use than are chains, being much lighter and more easily carried in the pocket. A necessary tool for making dog-leads is the hand punch, which is shown by Fig. 19, p. 16 of the companion volume " Harness Making "; for use with this a few nipples of different sizes should be obtained.

For hollow-studding the dog-leads, the hand-punch riveter, shown by Fig. 7, is required, the top piece being countersunk so that the stud top A just fits in. Fig. 8 illustrates a number of hollow studs. For riveting studs of different shape, obtain a few

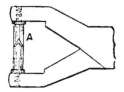

Fig. 7.—Hand-punch Riveter.

Fig. 8.—Hollow Studs.

of the top pieces A (Fig. 7) bored out exactly to fit the studs. Solid buttonhead rivets look extremely well, and can be hammered into the leather without previously making holes for their reception; for the latter reason they weaken the leather much less than do hollow studs. A screw-crease, as shown by Fig. 37, p. 19, of "Harness Making," is necessary for giving a gloss to the edges of the straps, etc.; the width of the mark made by it is regulated by the small screw, and the tool is heated slightly on the working part when required for use. Note that the working part alone requires heating; avoid heating the screw and thus making it useless. Practise with the tool on scrap leather before using it on good work.

The simplest kind of dog-lead will be described first, and this is illustrated by Fig. 9. To make it, first cut out a good leather strap from 36 in. to 50 in. long and about ½ in. or ¾ in. wide. Run the hot crease along the edges of the strap so as to make a bright mark; rub over and over again until the

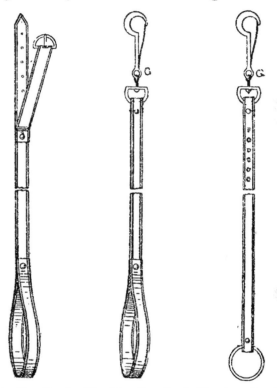

Fig. 9.---Dog Lead.　Fig. 10.---Dog Lead　Fig. 11.—Dog Lead
with Swivel.　with Studs and Ring.

required gloss is obtained. The hotter the crease, the smaller will be the pressure required, but care must be taken that it is not so hot as to burn and stick in the leather; a good plan is to heat the tool well, dip the working part in water, and use at once. Loop, and then rivet or sew one end of the strap to form a handle. Cut a ∧ on the other end of the strap, punch a few holes as shown, and rivet on a buckle strap; together with the buckle, this is 4½ in. long, and is creased or marked before riveting. This simple lead is now complete, and for use is buckled through the ring of the dog's collar.

In Fig. 10 is shown a better kind of lead, as the swivel G prevents it from twisting when the dog moves its head round. In making this dog-lead, proceed as before as far as the handle; in the event of the leather not being long enough to allow of this, cut a strap 12 in. to 18 in. long, loop it, and rivet it on to form the handle. Put the other end of the strap for about 1 in. through the swivel G, and rivet as shown. The lead is then complete.

A still better dog-lead is shown by Fig. 11; it differs from the last one in having, instead of a leather handle, a 1¼-in. or 1½-in. martingale ring passed through a loop at the end and secured by a rivet. The lead is then given a more finished appearance. Instead of the martingale ring alone, the chain-end fitting illustrated by Fig. 12 may be used. It is attached in the same manner as the plain ring. The dog-lead shown at Fig. 11 can be ornamented by any of the hollow brass studs shown by Fig. 8.

In putting in the studs, first with the punch make a number of holes at an equal distance apart. The necks B (Fig. 8) of these studs should fit tightly in the holes; when the studs are in the holes, with the rivet punch (Fig. 7) clinch their necks fast into the leather, the neck part being pressed outwards as in the section C (Fig. 8). D illustrates a stud having a rounded instead of a conical top.

Either brass or nickel-plated swivels will be suitable; the latter, perhaps, look the neater when new, but are more quickly tarnished than brass, and thus require more frequent cleaning. These remarks apply also to the martingale ring and chain-end fitting.

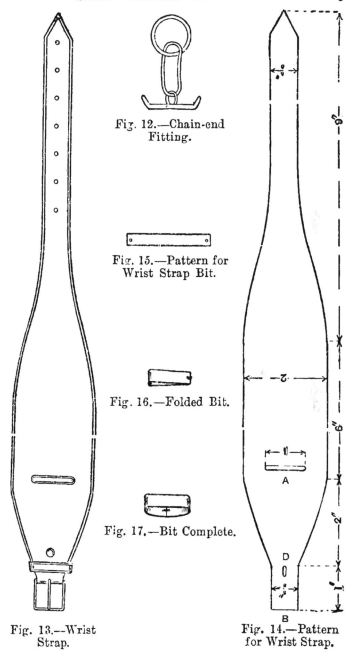

Fig. 12.—Chain-end Fitting.

Fig. 15.—Pattern for Wrist Strap Bit.

Fig. 16.—Folded Bit.

Fig. 17.—Bit Complete.

Fig. 13.—Wrist Strap.

Fig. 14.—Pattern for Wrist Strap.

The bifurcated rivets, used in fastening the different parts together, can be obtained nickel-plated, japanned, brassed, or coppered, as required, and are inserted and clinched with the aid of a hammer. Full instructions for doing this are given by the makers when sending out the rivets.

A strap for strengthening the wrist is shown in Fig. 13. First with a sharp knife cut a cardboard pattern to Fig. 14, and place it on a piece of thin, pliable leather, which may be of any colour required, though brown, stained, or enamelled looks the neatest. Mark carefully round the pattern with a lead pencil, and cut out just inside the pencil marks. Next, to cut out the slit A (Fig. 14), place the pattern on the leather, punch a small hole at each end of the slit, and cut out the piece between with the knife. The strap will be neater when finished if it is marked all round the edges (see Fig. 13) with a screw-crease.

Cut a piece of leather ¼ in. wide and 2 in. long, and on the centre line, near each end, with awl or punch make a small hole (Fig. 15); thread a piece of band through the two holes and tie it or sew the end. Cut the ends of the band close to the leather to Fig. 16, and bend the leather over, so that the jointed part is at the centre (Fig. 17). Put this bit on the end c (Fig. 13), then put the buckle tongue through the hole D (Fig. 14), bring the end B through the buckle and over the jointed part of the bit and sew down, or rivet with a bifurcated nickeled rivet. To finish, punch seven holes down the fastening part of the wrist strap. A nickel-plated buckle looks neatest.

In fixing, place the strap on the wrist; put the point through the slit A (Fig. 14) and pull until tight enough, then carry the end round again and buckle up, passing the point through the bit. The advantage of this wrist strap is that no buckle presses against the skin.

To make a pair of braces, first cut the web to a length of from 18 in. to 22 in., and, in the absence of brace-end punches, cut the pattern of the front strap to go to the buckle, and the hind piece to the button, and another to which the front buckle fastens. The front strap should be from 5 in. to 6 in. long. The back piece is about 3 in. long. Leave both pieces of the same width as the web in one end, and round it at the top, and mark a cross line as far as the webbing is to come; taper the other end of the strap, and round off the point.

Cut the back piece to shape from the points of the cross line, and taper it towrds the bottom, leaving it full opposite the intended buttonhole; cut the front buckle piece to the same shape at the bottom as the back piece, but narrow it towards the top to the width of the buckle. Turn in 1 in. at the top and cut a hole for the buckle; shave the point, crease, and finish all the straps, and stitch in the buckles with a loop close up to them. Have a piece of thin basil leather of the same size as, or a little larger than, the wide part in the strap end, and have back pieces from the cross line upwards.

Stitch along the cross line with single thread, and then put the web in as far as the stitches, and tack down. Having pricked the leather all round, stitch it in along the marks, trim the basil pieces, and cut them close round the stitches; punch the strap and a hole in the buckle-piece and in the back-piece about $\frac{1}{2}$ in. from the point, and slit the holes up for about 1 in.; the single end brace is now ready.

If the braces are to have cross straps in front (see Fig. 18) to fasten on two buttons, put a piece in the buckle of the same width all along and about $1\frac{1}{2}$ in. long. When doubled, stitch a loop near the buckle, leaving space below for the cross strap to go through; cut the cross-piece about 1 in. wide and 9 in. long and stitch it together in the centre with double thread ; narrow the other part a little, and taper to a point, letting it be a bit full opposite the hole.

Rub and crease it, and put the holes as directed in the other brace end, in the two ends of the cross strap, and then put them in the open space left at the bottom of the buckle-piece ; or this part may be made first and stitched in place while making the buckle part. Others, besides being double in front, join at the back (Fig. 19). Put both ends of the web together so as to cross, and insert a stitch or two

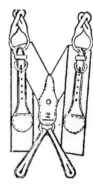

Fig. 19.—Double End Brace Joined at Back.

Fig. 18.—Double End Brace.

to hold them in their place ; bend a piece of leather, not too thick, and cut it neatly into the shape of an egg, pointed at the top to cover the joint, and narrow at the bottom where the bend is so as to take in a 1-in. dee or ring ; stitch it into the ring. Cut the back straps about $\frac{3}{4}$ in. wide, and narrow them gradually towards one end and round off the other. Turn down the narrow end for about 1 in., shave the point, and stitch to the dee previously stitched on. Finish by punching holes for the buckles.

In concluding this chapter the construction of a leather strap cutting appliance may be described. This will cut leather straps, belts, etc., of any thickness and length and up to 3 in. wide. To make the

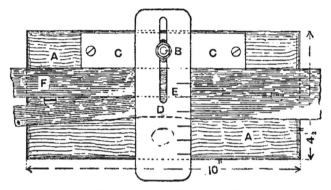

Fig. 20.—Strap Cutting Appliance.

appliances, first obtain a block (A, Fig. 20) about 10 in. long by $4\frac{1}{2}$ in. wide and $1\frac{1}{2}$ in. thick, of beech or any other hard wood, and round off the top edges as shown. Bore a hole about $\frac{3}{4}$ in. deep in the block from the underside to receive the head of a bolt $\frac{1}{4}$ in. by 2 in. long ; then bore the smaller part of the hole for the shank so that the block may lie flat on the table and the threaded part of the bolt come through A.

A sheet-iron plate (Fig. 21), 6 in. long by $1\frac{1}{4}$ in.

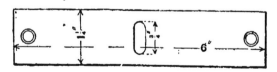

Fig. 21.—Plate of Strap Cutting Appliance.

wide and $\frac{1}{12}$ in. thick, will be required, with a slot about $\frac{3}{4}$ in. long in the centre to fit the bolt B (Fig. 20). A hole is bored and countersunk at each end for a small screw. Another piece of sheet iron D

(Fig. 20), 6 in. long by 2 in. wide and of any thickness, with a slot 3 in. long and $\frac{1}{4}$ in. wide, will be required to go on the bolt thread. Six slits or saw-kerfs, $\frac{1}{2}$ in. apart, $\frac{1}{2}$ in. deep, and wide enough for a knife blade to go through, are made in one edge as shown in Figs. 20 and 22.

To put the parts together, first take the sheet iron plate c (Fig. 20), put it on the bolt, and fasten to the block with a screw at each end. Then put the piece of sheet iron D on the bolt, leaving exactly the

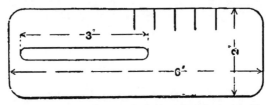

Fig. 22.—Another Plate of Strap Cutting Appliance.

width of the strap required to be cut between the edge of the plate c and a selected slit as E (Fig. 20). Screw the block to the table, and the apparatus is ready for cutting straps not thicker than the plate c (Fig. 20).

For cutting the straps, get a sharp knife, put the blade through the slit E (Fig. 20), and fix firmly in the wood block. Then take a piece of leather and press the edge against the knife until the cut end, F, comes through to the other side of the iron. Then pull the leather through with the right hand, keeping the edge of the leather firmly against the sheet-iron plate c with the left hand. The leather should come through easily, otherwise packing must be placed between the plates c and D. A nut and washer should be put on the sheet-iron plate D for tightening up, as shown in Fig. 20.

CHAPTER III.

LETTER CASES AND WRITING PADS.

THIS chapter will be devoted to instructions on making letter cases and writing pads, which have much in common. The first point to consider in making the leather letter case illustrated by Fig. 23 is the accurate cutting of patterns ; these, as shown in Figs. 24 to 28, would suit a case which, when open, is 8 in. by 6 in., and which, when closed, measures 6 in. by 4 in. Set out the patterns to the dimensions on thin cardboard or stout paper, and cut them out.

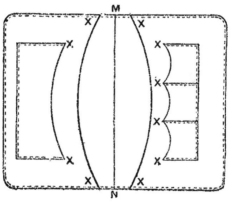

Fig. 23.—Letter Case.

After cutting the pattern for the back (Fig. 24), round the corner at A and fold the pattern in the centre, bringing A to B, and cut the same to it ; then fold again, bringing A and B to C and D ; this enables the worker to cut all corners to the same shape, the pattern being kept true and square. The side pockets (Figs. 25 and 26) can be cut in a similar way, rounding the corners at E and G to suit A and C

(Fig. 24), and J and L (Fig. 26) to suit B and D (Fig. 24). Prick the four holes in Fig. 25 in the position shown, and four similar holes in Fig. 26 ; these holes can be used as guides in fixing the card and stamp pockets. On Fig. 25 is stitched Fig. 27 to form a pocket for cards, Fig. 28 being stitched on Fig. 26 to form stamp pockets. Figs. 25 and 26 are stitched on the back (Fig. 24).

The most durable and suitable leather for making the case would be pigskin of medium substance, a firm piece being selected for the back. In cutting out, the pattern should be kept in position on the

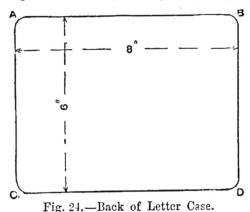

Fig. 24.—Back of Letter Case.

leather by a metal weight ; then with a blunt awl clearly mark the leather to the patterns, and with a shoemaker's knife or a pair of sharp scissors carefully cut the leather to the lines traced, endeavouring to keep clean edges. These should next be dyed to a shade similar to the leather, and this can best be done by using a sponge bound to a stick with string. After dyeing the edges, with a small quantity of grease on a rag rub them to a finish.

The stamp pockets (Fig. 28) must now be secured to Fig. 26, and to mark the position of the stitching a line should be made about $\frac{1}{8}$ in. from the outer edge of Fig. 28. This can be done best by running race compasses set to $\frac{1}{8}$ in. around the edges from o to P (see Fig. 23). Divide the pattern into three parts, and mark two lines inside for stitching. Take a small quantity of glue on the finger and

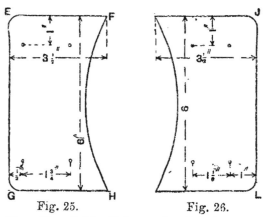

Fig. 25.   Fig. 26.

Figs. 25 and 26.—Patterns for Side Pockets.

smear it on the back of the leather from o to P about $\frac{1}{8}$ in. from the outer edge; then stick the piece to Fig. 26, bringing the points o and P on to the holes marked on Fig. 26. The holes are made by placing

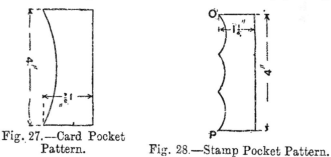

Fig. 27.—Card Pocket Pattern.

Fig. 28.—Stamp Pocket Pattern.

the paper pattern on the leather and pricking through with an awl.

Proceed in exactly the same way with the fixing of Fig. 27 to Fig. 26. A piece of linen or twill lining should be pasted at the back of Figs. 25 and 26 to

C

strengthen the stitching and prevent it breaking ; this must, of course, be done before stitching. After the patterns shown by Figs. 27 and 28 have been stitched to Figs. 25 and 26 all the stitching must be carefully tied and fastened off strongly.

Then glue around the back of Fig. 25 about ¼ in. from the edge, from F to H, and stick it on Fig. 24, bringing the points E and G over the points A and C. Do the same with Fig. 26, bringing the points J and L over the points B and D (Fig. 24). Next mark the back of the case for the stitching, making a line about ⅛ in. from the outer edge with compasses, and

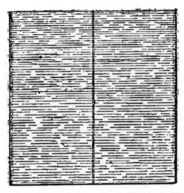

Fig. 29.—Writing Pad Folded Up.

running the line all round the back of Fig. 24. Then stitch and fasten off strongly at the corners of all pockets where marked with x (Fig. 23). If the outer edges overlap after the case is stitched, trim them with a sharp knife and dye and polish as before.

A piece of narrow elastic can now be stitched across the case in the centre at the points M and N (Fig. 25) ; this will be useful for keeping a diary or notebook in position. If the leather used is pigskin or cowhide, and it becomes soiled, the best way to cleanse it is by wiping with a weak solution of oxalic acid, and then, when dry, polishing with a soft rag.

The stitching can be done on a light Singer's, Thomas's, or vertical-feed sewing machine, using a No. 18 Pearsall's silk or a 60 in. thread. The stitch set should not be small, about twelve stitches to the inch being suitable. It is advisable to set and try the stitch on a waste piece of leather.

The writing pad illustrated by Figs. 29 and 30 has spaces for envelopes, notepaper, postcards, stamps, address book or diary, pen, pencil, scissors, eraser, and knife, and when open as shown in Fig. 30, the centre forms a blotting pad.

First cut a piece of leather 28 in. by 14 in., pare

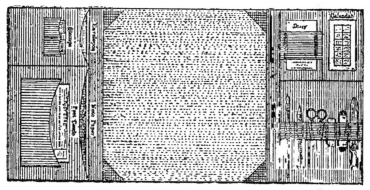

Fig. 30.—Writing Pad Open.

the edges all round, and mark the leather as shown at A, E, and D (Fig. 31). Then cut a piece of 1½-lb. strawboard 12 in. by 12 in., and with thin glue fix as shown at E, leaving 1 in. of leather to turn over at the top and bottom. Cut two pieces of strawboard 12 in. by 6 in., and glue at A and D, leaving 1 in. of leather between the boards and 1 in. at the sides to turn over on to the board. Then glue the 1-in. margins of leather to the board. This will form the groundwork for the pad. Pieces of twill lining, 11½ in. by 2½ in., should be cut and fixed at the bends at A E and E D (Fig. 31) to strengthen them.

Now cut a piece of leather 16 in. by 6¼ in., and

mark it as shown in Fig. 32 ; then cut pieces of cartridge paper and fix them as shown at x, and cut the
top of the leather the same shape as the paper,
leaving ½ in. of leather to turn over on to the board.
A piece of twill lining should be pasted at the back
within ¾ in. of the edge. Next turn the edge of the
leather to the lining and board ; fold the leather to
form gussets for the pockets, and, with the face of
the leather upwards, mark 1 in. from the edge at B,
next at 8¼ in., 9¾ in., 13¾ in., and 14¾ in. from the
edge. Glue together pieces of strawboard or soft
wood to form a mould for the paper pocket, 7¼ in. by

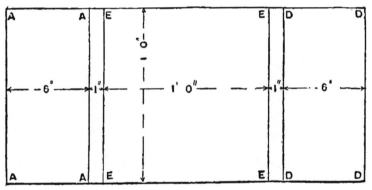

Fig. 31.—Base of Writing Pad.

4½ in., and for envelopes, 4 in. by 4½ in., and about
¾ in. thick, and round off the edges of the blocks.

In the next place cut a piece of cartridge paper
5 in. by 3 in., and shape as shown at o (Fig. 32).
Back this with lining, and fasten it on the leather,
leaving ⅜ in. to turn over all round. Pare the edge
and turn over to the lining and the paper, then cut
the paper and lining, 2½ in. by 1 in., to shape for
stamp pockets, and fix on the leather, leaving about
¼ in. to turn over all round. Pare the edge and turn
as before, lightly gluing the pockets at the edge,
and fix as shown in Fig. 32. These pockets should
be stitched at the three sides, as shown in Fig. 33.

Next cut a piece of ½-lb. strawboard 12 in. by 6 in., cover with linen, and fix on a piece of leather 12½ in. by 8¾ in., leaving about ¼ in. of leather all round, which should be turned over and stuck on the board, except where marked at A. 2 in. of leather is left to form the bend (see Fig. 33).

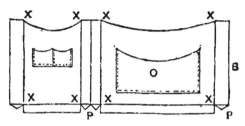

Fig. 32.—Writing Pad Pockets.

The paper and envelope pockets, with the stamp and postcard pockets stitched on, should be sewn as shown in Fig. 33. The ends and centre of the pockets should then be stitched, but not the bottoms. Cut the bottoms of the pockets as shown at P (Fig. 32), turn the two ears inside, and glue them to the bottoms. The piece of linen should next be cut

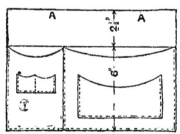

Fig. 33.—Writing Pad Pockets.

11 in. by 2 in., and glued at each bend at A E and E D in Fig. 31.

The pieces of leather with card and stamp, envelope and pockets for papers, should be glued and fixed at A (Fig. 31), across the bend and to the part that is to form the blotting pad. Care should be taken to fix the leather well in the bends and round each side, and also at the edges. Next cut a piece of board or thin cartridge paper about 9 in. by 1 in. ; back this with linen, and glue and fix it on a piece of leather $9\frac{3}{4}$ in. by 2 in., leaving $\frac{1}{2}$ in. margin of leather at each side and $\frac{3}{8}$ in. at the ends. Glue these margins and turn over to form loops.

Cut pieces of paper $2\frac{1}{2}$ in. by $1\frac{1}{2}$ in., and leather $3\frac{1}{4}$ in. by 3 in., and fasten in the same way for the diary. Next cut a piece of cartridge paper with linen at the back 4 in. by $2\frac{3}{4}$ in., and remove from the

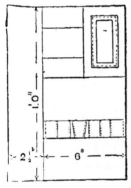

Fig. 34.—Writing
Pad Pockets.

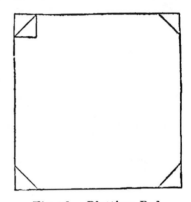

Fig. 35.—Blotting Pad.

centre a piece $3\frac{3}{8}$ in. by $2\frac{1}{3}$ in. Fix this piece in the centre of a piece of leather $4\frac{1}{2}$ in. by $3\frac{1}{4}$ in., and cut from the centre a piece $2\frac{7}{9}$ in. by $1\frac{5}{8}$ in. Pare the edges, turn over, and fix on the back of the frame. When this is fixed on the pad calendars can be slid in the spaces.

Now cut a piece of leather $12\frac{1}{2}$ in. by $8\frac{3}{4}$ in., and on it fix a piece of cartridge paper with linen at the back, 12 in. by 6 in., leaving $\frac{1}{4}$ in. of leather at the sides and one end. Loops for pens, scissors, etc., also diary and calendars, should be fixed and stitched as shown in Fig. 34. This should now be glued and fixed on in the position shown in Fig. 30.

A piece of strawboard 12 in. by 12 in. now is cut, and on it is pasted a piece of white watered paper, leaving ½ in. to turn over all round. This will form the foundation for the blotting pad. To make the four corners as shown in Fig. 35, cut four pieces of stiff paper 4 in. by 3 in., and four pieces of leather 4½ in. by 3 in. Pare the edges of the leather and stick it on the paper, turning ¼ in. of the leather over on one side.

Take a piece of wood about 3 in. square and ¼ in. thick, place it at the corner of the foundation for the pad as shown at the top left-hand corner in Fig. 35, then lay one of the pieces to form the corners on top of the wood at the distance given, the edge where the leather is turned over being on top. Glue the parts that overlap and fix them as shown, the wood acting as a mould for the corners. Fix the three other corners in the same manner, and cut away the parts that pucker, so as to form a flat surface under the pad. Next glue the foundation all over at the back and fix it firmly, as shown in Fig. 30.

If leather has been used the appearance can be improved if some fancy lines on the edges of the pockets and the fronts and back of the pad are made with a crease that has been slightly heated. Next take a small brush, and, with a small quantity of dye, black the edges of the leather where it may be showing white. If a polished leather has been used, coat it lightly with leather varnish. This should be applied with a fine hair brush or sponge. The leather most suitable to work would be a paste grain skiver.

CHAPTER IV.

HAIR BRUSH AND COLLAR CASES.

A GENTLEMAN'S hair brush case is a very useful requisite. It is easy to cut and make, and costs but very little. The brushes can be bought either singly or in pairs, and the case made accordingly.

Whatever kind of case is to be made, take a brush, lay it back downwards on a sheet of paper, hold it firmly, and mark it all round with a pencil; this will give the form A B D C in the diagram (Fig. 36). This can be doubled and quartered after it is roughly cut out, so as to get a good ellipse. Then take the thickness of the brush—or of the two, hair to hair, if the case is for a pair. Measure their circumference, and, whatever the length, cut the pattern about 1 in. longer and about $\frac{1}{4}$ in. wider. This is for the side and to form the lid, as E F G (Fig. 36).

With regard to the making there are only three pieces needed, without the buckle and straps, and these are described below.

The pattern must be folded across B C (Fig. 36) to get the half; two pieces should be cut to this pattern, and two holes pricked to indicate where the halves end. When they are faced together prick another hole at H. Round the portion at B A H run an iron (after damping the edge a little) to give it a finish. This may be a narrow, grooved iron, or the guard of a shoemaker's forepart or waist-iron will do, and after deducting the length of B D H (Fig. 36) from the side piece E F G, mark with this iron round the remainder, from H, passing F. A strap containing a few holes can be stitched on F, and a strap and buckle to match in a corresponding place on E, or the one at E can be left till after the case is made.

The leather may be lined, if desired, with brown or any coloured paper, and the edge of one of the ellipses may be placed against the end of the side at E and stitched, as B D C H, H being about 1 in. beyond the half at the back; and then the other side can be treated in a like manner.

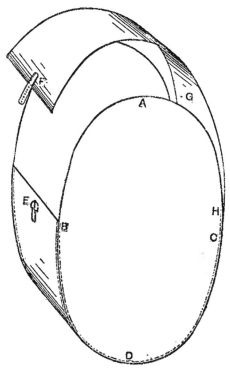

Fig. 36.—Hair Brush Case.

The brush case may be made of almost anything that is stiff and not too stout, as pieces from jockey tops, etc.; or where a fancy case is wanted, the pieces may be cut out in cardboard and then lined up with any thin leather, as Persian skiver, or any bookbinder's skivers, as morocco, roans, etc.; similar pieces are then cut out of whatever material is used for the outside. This may be some fancy embossed leather, about $\frac{3}{8}$ in. larger all round than the case is going to be. This, if not very thin in itself, must be skived all round for a little more than this distance, and then pasted and turned over the edge of the cardboard on to the other leather. If this is done nicely by skiving the edge very thin and taking small V pieces out all round previous to pasting, the edge will not need stitching. If it be

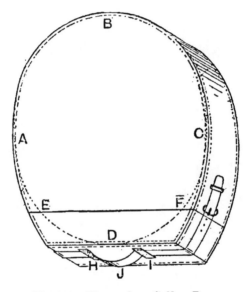

Fig. 37.—Horse-shoe Collar Box.

stitched use bookbinder's glue instead of paste. When these are thus fitted, all that is necessary is to proceed as above.

The threads may be of either white or yellow flax or hemp, and should be made wet and twisted, the tapers only being waxed to receive the bristles or needles; or they can be made from stout carpet thread of any colour. Tapers to this can be made by untwisting the ends after taking off the length wanted, and scraping each strand until it is tapered; then, when the whole are in this condition, wax and twist them, and put on the bristles or needles, according to the method of stitching to be adopted.

A horseshoe collar-box with drawer is shown by Fig. 37. The drawer can be used for handkerchiefs or ties, and for razor and tooth-brush also, if a partition is made along the side.

The form for the pattern is not difficult to obtain if the instructions given below are followed. First describe a circle as A B C D (Fig. 37); this, for a good-sized box, should be about 6 in. in diameter. Draw

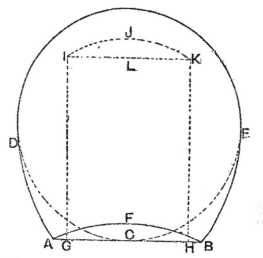

Fig. 38.—Forming Drawers in Collar Box.

a line as A B (Fig. 38), 4 in. long, touching the bottom of the circle at C; mark the points A and B 2 in. on each side of C. The curves A D and E B can then be drawn, thus forming the horseshoe. A curved piece can be taken away to save stuff, as F, and to give a little more play to the drawer.

Two of these patterns can be cut. A line is now drawn across the bottom as E F (Fig. 37), to form the lid—that is to say, if a piece of paper with a straight edge is put along this line and then cut round to the other parts of the pattern (except that it must be ¼ in. longer), the pattern for the lid is produced.

The height of the box should be from 3 in. to 3½ in. The pattern for it will, of course, be this height, and as long as the distance from A, past D and E to B (Fig. 38); two sides will be needed and a top for the lid. When a strap has been made as long as the distance from D to E, past A and B, the whole of the outside is complete.

As regards the drawer, it is best to draw two per-

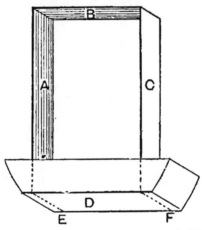

Fig. 39.—Collar Box Drawer and Lid.

pendicular lines, as G I and H K, each at right angles with c. These should be carried up as high as possible, say within about ¾ in. of any part of the outside circle, and they should be joined together either by the curved line I J K or the straight line I L K, the former for preference, as it gives more room to the drawer, for which there will be only one piece needed, either to C G I H, or to C D J H.

There must then be cut two sides and an end the length of I K. These are to form the portions shown in A, B, and C, in Fig. 39, the top of the lid forming the other end at D.

The piece for the sides of the drawer must be the

exact width of the inside of the box ; it is therefore best to leave this portion until the box is made. The lid being larger than the outside of the box, and the drawer having to go inside, the side of the drawer at A and B will not, of course, fit the lid at the dotted lines shown on top. It is not necessary, as a few stitches at E and F and along the bottom at D will hold it.

As regards the manufacture or the material used, these are explained in connection with the hair-brush case already described in this chapter.

Fig. 41.—Block for Making Collar Box.

Fig. 40.—Round Collar Box.

The strap which is to fasten either side may be put on merely from lid to box, just long enough to buckle, or it may be in one piece, as shown by the handle in Fig. 37, with holes in each end for the buckle to go through, and then secured in each of the places marked at H and I (Fig. 37), so as to form it into a handle, as J.

In making the drawer, it is as well to put the grain side of the leather inside and to cover the outside with nice paper ; the inside of the box should also be covered in a like manner to keep the collars clean. The drawer can, if desired, be made of wood. No lid will be needed, as the side of the box when the drawer is in forms this. At A and C (Fig. 37)

on the outside of the drawer are two elastic loops
to hold the collars in their place while the drawer
is being inserted.

Fig. 40 illustrates a round moulded collar case $6\frac{1}{4}$
in. in diameter by $3\frac{1}{4}$ in. high ; it is covered and lined
with leather. To make it, begin by cutting a circular
wood block (Fig. 41) $6\frac{1}{4}$ in. in diameter and $3\frac{1}{4}$ in.
deep, the surface of which should be smooth with
rounded corners. Cut a strip of moulding paper
about 22 in. by $4\frac{1}{2}$ in. and cut also two circular pieces
$6\frac{1}{4}$ in. in diameter. Glue the two ends of the long
strip on reverse sides for about $1\frac{1}{2}$ in. from the ends,
and then wind it tightly round the block, bringing
the glued edges over each other and joining them to
form the band of the case. Next place the band so

Fig. 42.—Catch Strap.   Fig. 43.—Hinge Strap.

that about $\frac{7}{8}$ in. overlaps at each side of the block.
Place one of the circular pieces on top of the block
and glue the $\frac{7}{8}$-in. of overlap to the circular pieces,
cuting out V-shaped pieces to get rid of puckers.

Carry out the same operation with the other circular piece at the bottom. The whole of the block
should now have been covered and a foundation
formed. Cut and add another piece of paper on the
top, bottom, and band as before, except that the
strip for the band should not be turned over on top
and bottom, and that the pieces should be glued all
over. Pieces of strawboard should be glued all over
and stuck on top and bottom and around the mould,
but the strip used for the bands should be pared at
the ends where they come together, so as to make a
neat finish.

The whole should be left to dry. Then with a

piece of glasspaper bound on wood, round off all the sharp corners, and roughen the surfaces so that the material will adhere better. The moulded part should now be cut. With a pair of compasses mark round the band about 1 in. from the top, and to this line with a sharp-pointed knife cut through to the block. The shallow part is for the lid and the other part for the case.

The leather or other material to be used for the case should next be cut as follows—One piece for the top of the lid $7\frac{1}{4}$ in. in diameter, one piece $\frac{1}{2}$ in. longer than the circumference and $2\frac{1}{4}$ in. wide, and one piece of the same length but 3 in. wide. If leather is used, pare or thin all the edges, and also the back and front of the ends of the long pieces to ensure a neat finish. The circular piece ($7\frac{1}{4}$ in. in diameter) should be fixed to the top of the lid with thin glue, leaving about $\frac{1}{2}$ in. of leather overlapping the edge to be turned over on to the band. Glue the strip $2\frac{1}{4}$ in. wide and fix the edge to the edge of the lid, neatly overlapping the two ends about $\frac{1}{4}$ in. The $1\frac{1}{4}$ in. of material left should be turned inside the lid.

The piece $3\frac{1}{4}$ in. wide should be fixed, like the lid, on the band of the case, leaving $\frac{1}{2}$ in. of material to turn over to the bottom and top inside the case. Next cut a piece the exact size of the bottom, pare its edge, and fix it on the outside of the case. The fastening should be fixed before lining the case, and a piece should be stitched at the back to form a hinge. First glue a piece of linen on some brown paper and cut two pieces to the dimensions given in Figs. 42 and 43. Then cut pieces of leather large enough to cover these, turning the leather over $\frac{1}{4}$ in. at each end and on the left side, and lastly $\frac{7}{8}$ in. on the right side, this making a neat finish.

An oblong catch or purse fastening about 1 in. by $\frac{3}{4}$ in. wide should be used. The hasp part of the catch should be fixed to Fig. 42, and the catch should be fixed to the body of the case so that the hasp falls in easily when the lid is closed. The piece of leather shown by Fig. 43 should be fixed at the back of the case (Fig. 44), directly opposite the catch in front, and secured at the bottom with another row of stitching about 1 in. above this, with one row at the top edge of the lid, and again $\frac{3}{4}$ in. below this.

The case should be lined. For this, cut two circular pieces of strawboard to fit inside, and one

Fig. 44.—Back of Round Collar Box.

strip of the same length as the circumference of the case inside and $\frac{1}{2}$ in. wider than the depth. Cut the material for the circular pieces about $\frac{1}{2}$ in. greater in diameter than the board, glue the same and fix on the board, turning $\frac{1}{4}$ in. over to the back of the board. Cover the strip of board and turn about $\frac{3}{4}$ in. of material over the edge. Pare the edge of the strip at the ends and glue the whole and fix it inside the case, bringing the edge where the material is turned over about $\frac{1}{2}$ in. above the top of the box, this forming a ridge to keep the lid in position. Next fix the two circular pieces in the lid and bottom of the case. If a polished leather has been used, lightly coat with leather varnish.

For leather varnish, place $2\frac{1}{2}$ oz. of powdered resin and 3 oz. of shellac in 1 pt. of methylated spirit; stir occasionally until dissolved, allow to settle, strain through canvas, and leave for twelve hours. The clear part should be used. Keep it corked up in a dry place.

CHAPTER V.

HAT CASES.

SOLID leather hat cases are made of good stout shoulders and first cuts, or, rather, the portions of a butt that take these names for other purposes; though, when they are going to be used for hat cases, they are specially dressed.

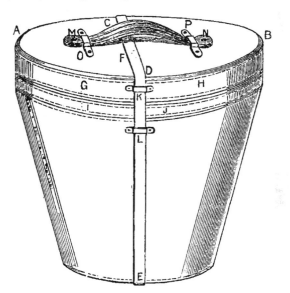

Fig. 45.—Bucket-shaped Hat Case.

Basil hat cases cannot be of solid leather, as basil is so thin that it has to be backed by stout millboards.

The diagrams given are for a bucket hat case. This is the most general shape, and it will take collars and ties, etc., as well.

Fig. 45 gives a back view of the hat case closed,

D

while Fig. 46 shows the front open, with portion taken away to show how and where the inner case, which is to hold the hat, is to go. The case must be oval, not round, and the top may be flat or curved (as A B C, Fig. 46). Directions for lining will be given, but this is done, of course, to taste.

Cut out the shape of all the pieces first in paper; then cut the leather to them, with as little waste as possible. For a curved top the dimensions of the

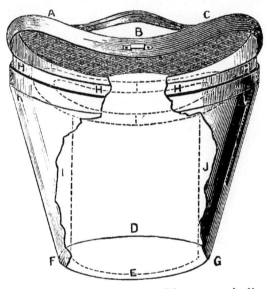

Fig. 46.—Hat Case shown Diagrammatically.

patterns are as follows: Top, cut oval (as A C B D, Fig. 45), 12½ in. by 13½ in. The bottom must be 8½ in. from D to E (Fig. 46), and 9½ in. from F to G. A strap is sewn at E (Fig. 45), and is 25 in. long from E, and goes past F and C, to lock on the front, and is 1½ in. wide. The sides of the case can be cut so that the seam comes under this strap, back and front. There will have to be two pieces cut to this pattern. The shape will be as Fig. 47, and the dimensions 15¼ in., A to B; 19½ in., C to D; 8¾ in., E to F; and 7 in.

from A to C and B to D. To form G H in Fig. 45, cut
four straight or slightly curved strips, 20½ in. by 2 in.
For the handle cut two pieces as Fig. 48, 10½ in. long,
1¾ in. wide in the centre, the ends being of any
shape and width desired.

A band for I and J (Fig. 45) may be cut as G H,
only narrower; this band is not necessary, but if
made, the width of it must be taken off the sides at
C F D (Fig. 47) to make up for it. Three strips about
3 in. by 1 in. are needed for loops K L (Fig. 45) and B
(Fig. 46). Take the two sides (Fig. 47), and fasten
them together at A C and B D, letting the stitches

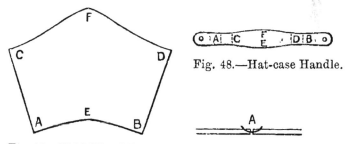

Fig. 48.—Hat-case Handle.

Fig. 47.—Half Side of Hat Case.   Fig. 49.—Sewn Seam.

be as the curved line at A (Fig. 49); this will give the
wall, or side of the case. Then shave off an angular
piece from all round the flesh side of the bottom, and
a corresponding piece from the inside of the bottom
of the pieces, which should be just seamed together.
Then turn upside down, and fit the bottom in, as A
on B (Fig. 50), and stitch it all round, as shown by
the line at C.

Now cut a piece of light millboard to fit the
bottom inside, and another piece to fit round the
side, twice the size of Fig. 47. Glue these together
at the side, at A C. The millboard should just nicely
fit in the case, and should be skived and allowed to
lap to make a smooth seam. Line this with red
glazed lining, 1 in. of which should be left at top
and bottom to turn over. Glue a piece of lining on

to the bottom board, leaving 1 in. over all round. Notch it all round about ½ in. apart, lay it on the bottom of the side lining, and glue it down. Then glue a strip 2 in. wide all round over this, letting half be on the bottom and half on the side.

While the lining is drying, take a strip of the board, 2 in. wide and curved to fit outside the top of the lining and inside the edge of the case, as H H H H (Fig. 46). Cover it with the lining, bringing the two edges to the bottom. Next damp the inside of the case, slightly glue it and the outside of the lining, and put it in its place in the case ; it will stand up about ¼ in. above the case. Now put the board rim between the two, letting it stand a good inch above the case, as shown by H H H H, and then stitch right through the lot. Sometimes the top edge of the case is bound with a narrow strip of thin leather, but it may be prepared and finished off without.

The lid is made in the same way, only the lining of the rim G H (Fig. 45), is not so thick, and the edge of the lining and edge of the rim must be flush with each other, and the top can be lined with quilted satin. Before the lining is inserted the handle must be put on.

To make the handle, take the two pieces (Fig. 48), put them together, and place two other pieces of the same material between them, letting one come from A to B, and the other from C to D, skiving or tapering them off at ends to nothing, and also skiving a litle off the edges at E F.

Only the top piece need be cut out to the shape desired, as the others can be trimmed to it after it has been stitched all round. After it is stitched and shaped, punch a hole in each end at M and N (Fig. 45), and put a brass-headed rivet in each. Do the same with two short, narrow straps which are to go across to stay the handle at O P ; or instead of using rivets all may be stitched down. This is for a fixed handle ; for a loose one, M and N will not want

punching, and must be a good deal wider. O and P
must then be well secured at each end to prevent
M and N slipping through; or pieces of brass, raised
in the centre just to admit of the thin part of the
handle passing backwards and forwards, may be
used. K and L may also be of brass, if desired; but
leather is more in keeping with the character of the
case, and is therefore worth the extra trouble. The
shape of these small leather or brass brackets is
shown at Fig. 51.

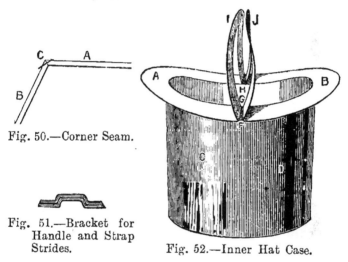

Fig. 50.—Corner Seam.

Fig. 51.—Bracket for
Handle and Strap
Strides.

Fig. 52.—Inner Hat Case.

The lock is put on the front, opposite to L
(Fig. 46), and its catch is riveted to the ends of the
strap. The lid does not come right off; and the
strap, between K and L, forms a loose sort of hinge.

The inner case (Fig. 52) is very simple, but should
be made to take a hat of any size. This is cut from
cardboard, and covered with the lining. Take a
piece of cardboard, $12\frac{1}{2}$ in. by $13\frac{1}{2}$ in. at least, and
from the centre cut a piece out, $8\frac{1}{2}$ in. by $7\frac{1}{2}$ in.; this
piece will form the bottom at Fig. 52, and the piece
that is left can be cut across the centre to form the
two half-rims, as A B.

The length of C D can now be ascertained by measuring round the piece which is to be the bottom. Only 1 in. can be left to form the seam, and the width of the inner case will have to be $7\frac{1}{2}$ in. This will be at A B ; but, after it is seamed up, it can be gradually cut down from these points at each side to a width of $6\frac{1}{2}$ in.

The inside of this inner case may be covered with the lining, which should be turned over to the outside, top and bottom. The bottom piece, covered on one side, as explained above, for the inside lining of the leather case, C D (Fig. 52), may now be covered outside. The lining should be turned round the top and over at the bottom, and a piece put over the bottom for a finish, and just stood in the case ; A and B should be trimmed at the sides to allow the inner case to fit inside the outer one.

The top of the sides may be covered with quilted satin, puffed a little with wadding, and finished off on the under side with lining. The quilted satin is only just secured on each side, which can be done by folding a piece of the lining and stitching it to the satin underneath F and the opposite side (letting A and B be $\frac{1}{2}$ in. apart), and about $\frac{3}{4}$ in. wider. This should be left on towards the centre, so that it may be stitched along the top of C D at G and H.

This must be done so as to leave A and B quite free to be lifted up, as shown at I J, so that when in the case collars, etc., can be put in the spaces between the inner and outer cases shown at I and J (Fig. 46).

A piece of $\frac{1}{2}$-in. elastic, with an old-fashioned garter-fastener in the centre, must be put across from K to L (Fig. 46) to hold the inner case containing the hat in its place.

CHAPTER VI.

BANJO AND MANDOLINE CASES.

A BANJO case, or a case for any similar instrument, can scarcely be made too well, as it often undergoes a lot of rough usage ; it fits so close to the instrument it is designed to protect, that, if badly made, or made of common or unsuitable leather, it forms a covering only, and is not really a protection. This chapter will therefore explain how to make a good, strong, solid leather case, such as, in fact, it would not be possible to buy at any shop, unless made specially to order.

It will be seen that in giving the patterns for the various parts of two different shaped cases, they are so placed together in Figs. 53 and 54 as to enable them to be cut from a strip of leather with the least possible waste—an important consideration in cutting up leather. First measure the banjo, or lay it on a sheet of paper, and cut the bottom pattern to it, as A, in Fig. 53, leaving, of course, a margin all round ; and then cut the other parts, as there shown, placing them together in a like manner. It will now be seen how much stuff will be required.

The height of the banjo must be ascertained to determine the thickness of the case ; the smaller all parts can be got, the better will be the fit and the cheaper the case.

As a good illustration of the shapes and their positions given in the diagrams, only a few hints will be needed as to the method of making it.

Suppose the work is done from measurements. Take the exact length of the banjo, the width of rim including brackets, height of highest portion as it lies upon a flat surface, and the width of the key-

board. Letting the rim measure be the diameter,
describe a circle to it; take from a portion of this
circumference the width of the keyboard, then draw
two lines the length of the handle, as M N; the
length of these can be ascertained by drawing the
length of the banjo as O L, and making the M and N
meet the line L. This done, allow $\frac{1}{4}$ in. all round,
and cut out this, the bottom pattern; then cut
another to it, but $\frac{1}{8}$ in. longer, for the lid.

Cut B the width of the measurement previously
alluded to as the height, and the length can be
found as follows: Suppose the width of rim to be
12 in., the circumference would be about 36 in.;
B would therefore be this length less the distance
between M and N. And the same rule will apply to
F for the rim of the lid, but it will be longer, as the
circumference is larger. The length of the two
sides can be obtained by measuring from P, past N
and Q, to L, where these two (C and D) may join; and
this rule will again apply to G and H for the lid; or
they need only be cut the length of P to Q, and a
piece joined on the end (at each corner) as I. The
handle J can be cut to any shape desired, and can
easily be cut from the spare corner shown. This
completes all the outer pieces for the case shown
in Fig. 55.

The whole of the inside of the banjo case may be
covered with any coloured baize or flannel, the
edges of which should be turned in so that it is just
a shade smaller than the above patterns. This lining
should be glued into its place after the case is made.
The stitches in nearly the whole of these cases are
made as shown in Fig. 56. This is not at all difficult, and can be done either with harness-makers'
needles or with a thread as used by shoemakers;
the latter is the stronger, as only a very small hole
is needed.

The small box for strings, etc., may be made
from stout cardboard, and covered with the lining;

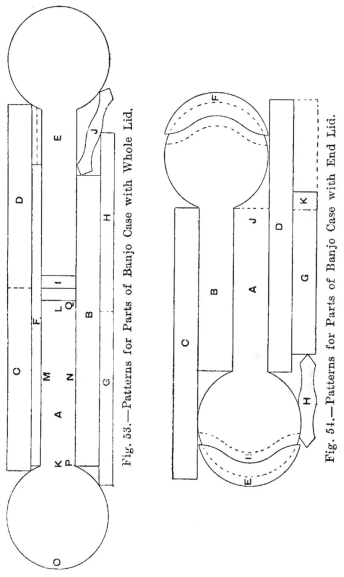

Fig. 53.—Patterns for Parts of Banjo Case with Whole Lid.

Fig. 54.—Patterns for Parts of Banjo Case with End Lid.

it is put in in the same way, and can, of course, be fastened with buckles and straps, clasps, or lock and key, though if properly fitted it may be left without. The piece taken out between A B (Fig. 55) is to receive the finger when the box is being opened.

The handle may be stitched on or fastened by two copper rivets at C and D. Two straps and buckles, one at E and another at F, will hold on the lid, which may be fastened with lock and key, clasp, or another strap and buckle.

The banjo case shown in Fig. 57, of which Fig. 54 gives the parts in section, is a very handy shape, and is a little cheaper to cut.

In this case the top and bottom are the same size and shape, as shown by A and B. The pattern should be obtained in the same way as before, but it will

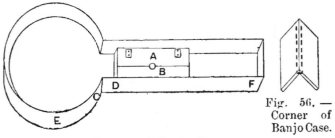

Fig. 56. — Corner of Banjo Case.

Fig. 55.—Bottom of Banjo Case.

not need to be quite so long—that is to say, only from I to J (Fig. 54). It will be seen, by reference to Fig. 57, that the lid should cover only about 2 in. of case as at A. It will be found that about 2 in. or more in the sides of the lid can be saved by cutting, as here shown, some of the one out of the other, as F and E (Fig. 54). The other sectional parts of this illustration are the two sides C and D, and E and F, the top and bottom of the lid ; G, the side of the lid, and H the handle.

The dotted lines in A and B show how a pattern of the lid can be obtained, the outer one being cut to the portion of the circle it is to cover, and the inner ones to any shape you wish, but the narrower it is

at E and I the more economical the cutting. C and
D should be cut long enough to form the whole of
the sides and the end, as each shown here will come
from B to C (Fig. 57). G, in Fig. 54, is for the rim of
the lid, and is cut about 2 in. or 3 in. longer than
the lid ; this end is left on one side, to be stitched
to the case at D (Fig. 57), and forms a good hinge.
H, in Fig. 54, is the handle, and should be attached
to the case as shown above. The remaining pieces
will be needed for buckle-straps and loops.

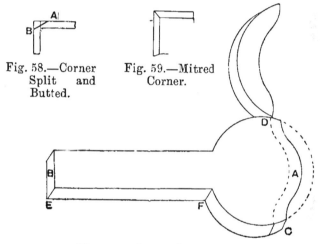

Fig. 58.—Corner
Split and
Butted.

Fig. 59.—Mitred
Corner.

Fig. 57.—Banjo Case with End Lid.

Where the leather is required to be turned to an
angle, as at E (Fig. 57), a piece must be taken out of
the leather about halfway through on the wrong
side ; and when one is required as at F, give one
straight cut halfway through ; they can then be
tapped down on an angular piece of wood.

Another very good way of making the seams at
the corners is to take the top and bottom, or all the
sides, and draw a line all round with a pair of compasses about $\frac{3}{16}$ in. in from the edge, and from this
line make holes all round ; put the point in at this

line, and bring it out at the edge of the leather
about two-thirds of the way through, as shown by
A in Fig. 58. It will now be seen that B is the other
piece of leather, and that when the two are put
together to form a corner, as A and B, and while A
is butted against B, the awl is put in at A and pushed
through till it comes out at B. This makes a very
solid corner.

In putting this banjo case together, it must be
lined up first, care being taken to line it firmly, as
it cannot be done afterwards without undoing the

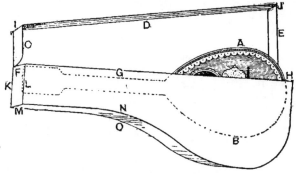

Fig. 60.—Mandoline in Case.

stitches. Strings, etc., should be kept in a small
box covered with baize, which should be placed inside the banjo prior to putting it in the case.

For the above the leather is cut and enough stuff
allowed to admit of an angular piece being taken
off all the corners, so that the portions which are to
be stitched can be laid together as in Fig. 59.

The method of making a mandoline case in
American cloth, with bound and turned-in edges,
will now be explained; the method to be adopted
when leather is used will be self-suggestive.

In Fig. 60 at A is given a portion of the body of
the mandoline standing out of the case, to show
how it is put into the case and the way the case is
made. Looking at a case of this shape it might be

thought that the mandoline is put in so that the strings come next to the lid, whereas it is laid in on its side, one side being at the bottom, as shown by the dotted lines B.

The method of cutting the pattern will depend on the size and exact construction of the mandoline ; but by way of example the sizes in inches of various parts at different points of a case for an ordinary mandoline are given. These dimensions will require slightly modifying for instruments of other shapes and sizes.

Take a piece of paper, the left-hand top corner of which must be a right angle, as A (Fig. 61). Mark a point at C along the top 24½ in. from A ; draw C D

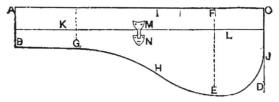

Fig. 61.—Elevation of Mandoline Case.

at right angles to A C, and E F parallel to C D at a distance of about one-fifth of the distance from A to C. Make F E 8¼ in. long. A line is drawn from A to B, which should be 3¾ in. long, and another drawn from B to G—that is about a quarter of the length, and parallel with A C. From this point draw the curve G H E J. From H to I the distance will be about 5½ in. The point J, where the curve ends, is about 4 in. from C, on the line C D. The line K L should be about 2 in. long, and indicates the edge of the rim of the lid.

The next pattern is the top of the lid, 24¾ in. long from A to B (Fig. 62), 6¾ in. from C to D, and 3¼ in. from E to F. The next is for the bottom. This is cut in the same way as for the lid, only, as it has to go round the curves, it will need to be 32¼ in. long from A to B (Fig. 63). C D must be $6\frac{5}{8}$ in., and E F $3\frac{1}{8}$ in. long. The end piece is next cut; this should be $3\frac{3}{4}$ in. by 3 in., as shown in Fig. 64, while the handle should be cut as shown in Fig. 62 at G. Two

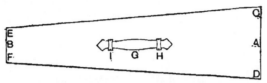

Fig. 62.—Top of Mandoline Case.

pieces the same width as A C K L (Fig. 61), one the length of C D, the other of E F (Fig. 62), are required, and the whole of the patterns are cut.

To each of these patterns cut pieces of stout strawboard—one to each piece—excepting Fig. 61, to which two pieces must be cut. These, when the whole are cut, may be temporarily fastened together in their proper places by strips of gummed paper, in order to test their correctness, and the mandoline should be tried to see if it fits before finishing the making of the case. If everything is satisfactory, put a mark on the outside of each piece so that they may not get mixed.

It is best to line the insides first. This can be done with baize, striped union, or any material or colour preferred, and this may be stuck on with

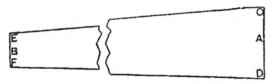

Fig. 63.—Bottom of Mandoline Case.

bookbinders' paste. Take one side, as Fig. 61, and the lid (Fig. 62), and lay them with their widest sides together, so that they are about $\frac{1}{4}$ in. apart, not more. Paste the lining on to these and let it dry;

serve the inside of each piece the same, doing these
one at a time ; then pare the edges of the lining off
to the edge of the board, except in the first instance,
where the lid and side are joined together.

Now the outside is covered in the same way with
American cloth, and trimmed off at the edges, if the
edges and corners are to be bound, as will be explained later. If they are only to be stitched
through (a very nice, neat way), the American cloth
is left on $\frac{1}{2}$ in. all round, pasted, and turned over on
to the lining. When done in this way, the corner
seams should be made as Fig. 65 at A, letting B and
C be the stitch, which is set right through to catch
the edges of everything. This would also mean

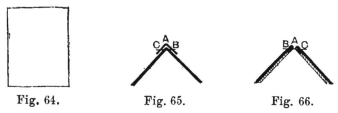

Fig. 64.   Fig. 65.   Fig. 66.

Fig. 64.—Mandoline Case End Piece. Fig. 65.—Binding
Corner of Case. Fig. 66.—Stitching Corner of Case.

stitching or felling all the other edges down, as on
the lid, at C, D, E (Fig. 60), and also the three edges
of the body at F, G, and H.

The lid and one side may be covered at the same
time, and if the lining and the outer covering are
pasted well together, they form a good solid hinge
for the lid, which is much better than having a
movable lid. The corners that will have to be
stitched through are I, J, K, L, M, N, and O (Fig. 60).

If the lining and covering has been done with a
raw edge, a long strip of basil or persian, about
$\frac{3}{4}$ in. wide, must be damped and folded down the
centre, grain side out. Lay this on the corners, as
A (Fig. 66), put the awl in at B, and bring it out at C,
so that it catches all the edges in the stitching.

Another long strip will then be needed for the binding of the plain edges. This will need to be only ½ in. wide, but it may be wider if desired. It must be lapped over the edges C, D, E (Fig. 60), and also F, G, H, and the awl put in at one edge of the binding and brought out at the other, near each edge, but the stitching must catch both edges. It is best to put these on so that there is no join at the corners, as for instance at F and H, as it will help to keep the body and lid in shape and thus make it more durable. If it is wished to make a better or prettier cover, instead of using American cloth, use thin leather, as patent seal, etc., or a fancy stamped roan.

The handle is put on at H and I (Fig. 62) with leather or brass slides. The case may be fastened with a spring or ordinary lock, letting the lock be on the case, as N (Fig. 61), and the hasp on the lid as M. On the back, under the lid, inside at O (Fig. 60), there will be a space at the back of the neck or handle of the mandoline. This can be made use of, as a little box could be fitted here to carry string, etc.; or two narrow straps, some little distance apart, may be affixed to take a small pocket-book; and just above the same place, on the lid, a narrow strip may be stitched on, well fastened at each end with a stitch here and there, about ½ in. apart, to put the plectrums in.

If the case is made of American leather cloth, the stitches need not be very short—say three to the inch—and the thread may be made from stout carpet thread, with tapers made as has been explained and fastened on to harness-makers' needles, and the holes made with a flat, diamond-shaped awl.

See that the case is quite dry before the mandoline is put into it, or the steel strings will be injured.

CHAPTER VII.

BAGS.

THIS chapter will deal with the methods of making leather bags of five chief kinds—brief, lady's hand, Gladstone, and tennis. This by no means exhausts the subject, but the bags chosen are representative, and, following the instructions given, it should not be difficult to make a bag of any other shape after thoroughly examining it.

The two most useful sizes for brief bags are undoubtedly 12-in. and 14-in. Like Gladstone bags and some other kinds, the difference in length be-

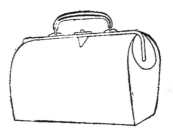

Fig. 67.—Brief Bag.

tween any two consecutive sizes of brief bags is generally 2 in. The sizes usually kept in stock are 10 in., 12 in., 14 in., and 16 in., but any size under, above, or between these can be obtained to order.

In width and depth brief bags differ considerably. In those 12 in. long the width of the bottoms varies from $3\frac{1}{4}$ in. to $5\frac{1}{2}$ in., and in 14-in. bags $\frac{1}{2}$ in. excess over these measures is allowed, the difference in depth being in proportion; the sides of the smallest size measure anything between 7 in. and 10 in., and in the other $7\frac{1}{2}$ in. to $10\frac{3}{4}$ in. It being always easier to reduce than to enlarge a pattern,

E

and more convenient generally to have a bag slightly too small, the dimensions given in this article will be the largest, in proportion to the length, and may be reduced as desired.

Fig. 68.—Narrower Brief Bag.

Fig. 67 shows a bag well proportioned ; Fig. 68 is much narrower at the bottom, and not so deep.

The way to cut out the patterns for either of these bags is to open the frame as in Fig. 69, and lay it perfectly flat on the bench, and with a rule measure it carefully between the corners A A and B B. The frame will be found to be slightly less at B B, owing to this part closing into the other half, and the difference must be allowed for in cutting out the leather. In both bags the distance between G G (Fig. 70) and D D (Fig. 71) is the same.

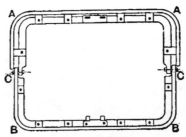

Fig. 69.—Brief Bag Frame.

The dimensions in the diagrams are given for a 12-in. bag, and will measure 12 in. by 10 in. by 5 in. when finished. A bag is always measured at the frame, and the length of the bottom should always be 1 in. more than this. Get a sheet of thin brown paper, and fold it in the middle. Mark it correctly the exact depth and half the distances between G G and H H, and cut through the double paper. This

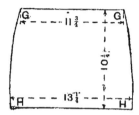

Fig. 70.—Pattern for Side of Bag.

ensures both sides of the pattern taking the same curve at the swelled part.

The pattern in Fig. 70 is for the sides, and should measure along the top 11¾ in., and at the bottom 13¼ in. Next measure the frame from A to B for the gusset (Fig. 71). The distance will be found to be 8 in. ; but if closed it will be quite 8½ in., the hinge of the frame making this difference. Therefore cut the gusset 8½ in. from D to D, 10 in. from E to E, and 5¼ in. at the bottom, F F. The depth of the gusset will be 10 in. only. Then, when the seams D F and

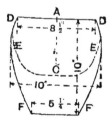

Fig. 71.—Gusset Pattern.

Fig. 72.—Gusset Stiffening Pattern.

G H are made, all ends will be level. The pattern for the bottom will measure 13¼ in. by 5¼ in. All seams are allowed for.

To cut out the bag, lay the leather on the bench,

grain side down, and see that the patterns are placed on it so that the grain marks will all run in the same direction when the bag is made up. Cut out the sides first, and, as they are more exposed than any other part, they should be taken from the best part of the leather.

Take the gussets next, then the bottom; the welt pieces may be cut from the thinnest part of what is left.

Begin sewing the bag by taking one of the sides and one gusset. Place them face to face, so that D and G and F and H meet respectively, placing a welt piece between the edges, and stitching with a good waxed thread made of four-cord No. 9 patent

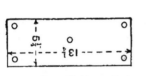

Fig. 73.—Bag Bottom Pattern.

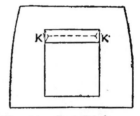

Fig. 74.—Bag Lining and Pocket.

hemp. When the four seams joining together the sides and gussets are finished, sew in the bottom, putting a welt piece in these seams also.

The bag will now be ready for turning, and the corners must be well worked out and tapped down with a hammer previous to putting in the stiffenings.

For the side stiffenings take an 8-oz. strawboard, and cut two pieces $\frac{1}{4}$ in. less all round than the pattern used in cutting out the leather. The bottom stiffening will be about $12\frac{3}{4}$ in. long by $4\frac{3}{4}$ in. wide, and must be cut from a 2-lb. strawboard. Fig. 72 shows the pattern for stiffening the gussets. Cut this from a 16-oz. strawboard. The bottom stiffening must be glued in first, and the studs put through and fastened down as in Fig. 73. See that the stiffening fits firmly every part within the seams, and rub it well down with the rubbing bone before the glue sets.

In cutting out the gusset stiffenings, the distance from A to C when they are in position as shown by dotted lines (Fig. 71) must be rather more than the distance from A to C on the frame (Fig. 69). If the glue should show signs of setting too rapidly, a teaspoonful of treacle added to $\frac{1}{2}$ lb. of glue will be found effectual. Use a large brush, hot glue, and get the stiffenings into position quickly.

For covering the frame, take a nice thin piece of hide (persian works better), cut a strip 20 in. long by 4 in. wide for covering the largest half, and another strip 19 in. long by $2\frac{1}{4}$ in. wide for the other half. The frame in this case will be covered all over, as shown in Fig. 68, and the edges of the covering must be brought to that side of the frame which will be out of sight when the bag is finished. Use good paste, and fix the key-plate and handle-plates in position before pasting the covering to the under side of frame. The method of making the handle and fixing the plates to the frame, besides much other useful information, is given when describing how to make a Gladstone bag (see pp. 73 to 83).

Any kind of lining—roan, skiver, or linen twill—may be chosen, and in cutting it out of the same patterns used for the outside will do. A pocket must be formed on one of the sides, as shown in Fig. 74. To do this, cut the lining as shown by dotted lines K K, and finish at each end in the form of the letter V   The edges thus produced are pasted down inside ; this makes a good opening to the pocket. A piece of material like the lining is put on to the back, cut large enough to receive the stitching, and the pocket is formed by stitching the three sides and above the opening for the same.

When the lining is finished, place it inside the bag, pocket side opposite the lock, and glue to the bottom and round the top of the bag. Trim off any excess of lining here, and prepare to sew the bag to the frame. Start at one of the corners, either A or B, and fix on a tab when sewing B side, to open it by. See that all seams meet before starting to stitch, and use black flax in making threads for this part. At x (Fig. 68) a fulness of the gusset is shown, which must be made in framing this part; this allows the bag to close easily, as before mentioned, and causes no strain to the hinges.

The frames, as well as the material, for making ladies' bags are very different from those used in making brief bags, and there is a much greater variety of each. For instance, ladies' bags are made in russia, roan, morocco, pressed grains, and leather cloth, besides many special kinds of fancy leathers and other materials. There is also quite a variety of frames used, from the plain japanned to the elaborate nickel or gilt, with mounts to correspond.

In buying a frame it will be advisable to get a few pins with it for riveting the parts together.

If an old bag is at hand the same size and style as the one it is desired to make, take patterns of all the parts, then lay them in order on a large sheet of paper, to serve as a guide in selecting a skin of suitable size. Take care not to buy too small a skin, or one which would leave a lot of surplus on hand.

Morocco, roan, or russia bags are usually lined with leather. This may be either persian or a good skiver, either of which may be obtained in fancy colours. For a single bag, a small persian would perhaps be the most economical to buy. The largest pieces for the bag should be cut out first, and from the best part of the skin.

The sizes of pieces required for a 10-in. square pattern bag are as follow: One piece, 17 in. by 10 in., forming one side, bottom, and pocket on the other side. The flap which completes this side is cut 6 in. by 10 in. Four pieces for the stiffened portion of the ends must be cut 6 in. by 2 in. each, and the flexible portions forming the gussets $6\frac{1}{2}$ in. on each side, $5\frac{1}{2}$ in. at the top, and 1-in. only at the bottom. The shape of these two pieces is almost triangular. One 2-in. by 6-in. piece is laid on each $6\frac{1}{2}$-in. side, and the parts are stitched together, leaving the $5\frac{1}{2}$ in. to be riveted to the frame, and the 1-in. part for seaming to the bottom of the bag.

A piece of American cloth is generally used for that side of the bag covered by the flap and pocket. Narrow strips of leather of the same kind as that used for the bag are stitched on each side of this to prevent the cloth being seen beneath each end of the flap. These must be cut 1 in. wide by 5 in. long, and must be stitched to the cloth before the side seams are made. The flap is made up quite separately from the bag. The lower corners of this are slightly rounded, and a piece of American cloth is cut the same size for the back and to provide the casing for the springs to slide in.

The spring pieces are cut $\frac{7}{8}$ in. wide by 3 in. long, and good black elastic, $\frac{3}{4}$ in. wide, is stitched to one end of each, the other end of the leather being rounded and the fastener riveted on to it. The counterpart of this fastener—or stud—is riveted on to the pocket. The flap must be neatly bound with thin leather cut $\frac{5}{8}$ in. wide, which provides a good surplus for the underside, and ensures the stitching taking a good hold of the bottom edge. All the stitching may be done by any domestic sewing machine, as the material is in no case very heavy. The lines on the flap are creased with a tool, referred to in previous chapters, heated and worked along in a straight line.

In seaming the body and ends of the bag together, place a narrow welt piece between them, so that when the bag is turned the welt will show.

When the bag has been turned, stiffen the bottom
and sides as directed, and put four nickel clamps
or nails in the four corners of the bottom. The
leather of the flap should also be stiffened with good
brown paper before being made up.

To rivet the frame to the bag, fix the four
corners first, the flap being put in with the rest, and
on the same side of the frame as the pull-piece to
the lock catch. The lining is also riveted in at the
same time. This lining is not cut the same as the
outside leather, but in three pieces only—one piece
is cut the full width of the bag, and extends from
the frame on one side to the other. The ends or
gussets are each in one piece. The elastic springs
should also be stitched at the top of the flap to
prevent pulling away in use.

Two plates of metal are sold with each frame—
in fact, form a part of it—to hide the cut edges at
the top of the bag, and also to receive the burr
formed in riveting the pins. These are made exactly
the same shape as the frame itself.

For riveting the parts together a few tools are
essential, but these are not very expensive ; they
include a fine round awl for piercing the leather in
passing through the pins, a pair of small wire
cutters such as are used by watchmakers, and a
1-oz. hammer. In the bag trade special irons are
used for riveting on, but an excellent substitute
will be found in a small iron foot (such as is used
in boot repairing) supported by a suitable stand.

Having fixed the four corners so that the seams
on each side meet perfectly, pass the pins through
the holes near the hinges and rivet them ; then
through the holes near the lock and catch, and complete it by working alternately on each side of these.
Do not leave too much metal for burring down, or
the pins will bend, and fresh ones will have to be put
in ; also avoid cutting them too short to form a head.
The " toe " of the iron foot is placed under each pin-

head, and the bag held in a horizontal position whilst being riveted.

Handles for ladies' bags are always made much longer than for other bags, to permit of their being carried on the arm. The usual length is 10 in. Cut two pieces of leather, each 10 in. by 1 in. Stout cord covered with brown paper is used as a filling. Cut a piece of paper, 10 in. wide, wet it, lay the cord evenly along one end, and begin to roll the cord within the paper.

A perfectly level table or bench is the best for rolling it on. Be careful to get the first few turns tight, then place the hands on the roll and keep working it until it is quite firm; then lay on one side to dry. The tapering ends are made by peeling off a portion of the paper, commencing at the middle, and increasing as the ends are neared. Paste the leather covering over this, so that the edges meet evenly on each side; then stitch and trim them. Pare the ends before placing them in the fittings attached to the frame, and secure them in their places by passing through a pin and riveting its end.

Of Gladstone bags the most convenient size for ordinary use is the 22 in. one. This will hold a coat or a pair of trousers folded once over; with an 18-in. or 20-in. bag two folds generally have to be made. Much larger sizes prove very cumbersome to carry.

Two of the chief evils to which a Gladstone bag is liable are (1) a broken frame and (2) unstitching of the seams. The first of these is caused, in nearly every instance, by careless usage; the second may be due to common thread being used in joining the parts together. Nearly all kinds of bags are machine sewn, and chiefly with very thin thread; black bags are sewn with a thread of that colour, which soon becomes rotten, owing to the dye used in its manufacture. It is very essential, in making a bag, to use a good waxed thread for the seams to ensure the work being permanent.

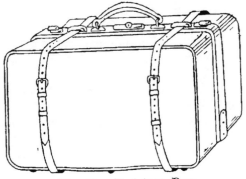

Fig. 75.—Gladstone Bag.

Cheap leather should not be used, for not only do the frame and fittings cost the same, but the cheap material requires more care and skill in its

Fig. 76.—Another Gladstone Bag.

manipulation; moreover, it will not last a quarter the time that one made of good leather will. Very few brown bags are waterproof; and sometimes, after being out in a drenching rain, a brown bag will be so sodden with wet that it takes a long time to get dry, and the stiffening curls or comes away in places, causing an unsightly appearance. With enamelled cowhide there is not this risk, and, when used with care, it will preserve its glossiness for years.

Fig. 75 shows a Gladstone bag with full fittings. A indicates lock and plate; B, handle plates; C, strap loops; D, slides; E, shoes. A 22-in. frame with these fittings costs 2s. 6d. Fig. 76 shows the interior of a bag with the necessary straps, etc.; this bag has a lock at each end of frame, and has no slides.

Strawboard in three different weights will be

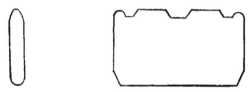

Fig. 77.—Rubbing Bone or Stick.

Fig. 78.—Stiffening for Bag Division.

required; it costs 1d. per lb. One 2-lb. board for the bottom, about four 16-oz. boards for stiffening the sides and cutting patterns, and two 8-oz. for stiffening the bands. Six nails to protect the bottom; 2 1-in. buckles for outside straps; half dozen $\frac{5}{8}$-in. buckles for inside straps; a ball each of brown, yellow, and black flax; and 3 yds. of twill lining will also be necessary.

A few simple tools will be required—a clamp to hold the work for sewing (the worker can make these as explained in Chapter I. of " Harness Making "); two or three different sized awls in handles; a pennyworth each of No. 1 and No. 4 harness needles; a clicker's knife; and a bone the same shape as Fig. 77 for rubbing down the stiffenings.

If this latter cannot be obtained, a piece of hard, straight-grained wood, filed to shape, answers the purpose nearly as well. The glue brush should be quite 2 in. in diameter at the band. A paint brush thoroughly cleaned will do, but every particle of paint must be washed out. A gluepot of suitable size for the brush—say, a No. 4 or No. 5—can be bought at any large ironmonger's.

In making the Gladstone bag, the first thing to do is to get out the patterns. Take one of the 16-oz. strawboards, lay the closed frame on it, and mark evenly round and along the wire at the bottom. Cut this out with a large pair of scissors, and the pattern for the sides is ready. The pattern for the bottom must be $21\frac{1}{2}$ in. by 9 in. For the division

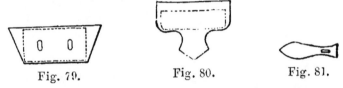

Fig. 79.   Fig. 80.   Fig. 81.

Fig. 79.—Leather Pocket. Fig. 80.—Pocket Flap. Fig. 81.— Buckle Chape.

board, cut a pattern $\frac{1}{8}$ in. less all round than the pattern for the sides, and shape it as in Fig. 78 if a frame with single lock and slides is used. A pattern for the pocket (Fig. 79), and one for the flap (Fig. 80), must also be cut, and if fancy buckle chapes (Fig. 81) are used, a pattern of these should be cut.

In cutting these smaller patterns, it is a good plan to cut one first by folding a piece of thin paper (Fig. 82, pocket-flap pattern folded); mark and cut it so that when it is opened both sides of the pattern are alike. Paste this on to the straw-board, and cut evenly round the edge of paper. Fig. 83 is a pattern for the middle piece in the handle.

In beginning to cut out the bag, take the side

pattern, lay it on the leather, and see that both sides can be got out with the grain running in the same direction. Use a sharp knife, and if a level board large enough is not handy, lay one of the strawboards under the leather and cut out on that. Cut quite close to the pattern, guiding the knife with the finger pressed against it and the edge of the pattern. See that there are no flaws or blemishes under the pattern, or they will be sure to show when made up. The bands will need to be 45 in. long, one by $6\frac{1}{4}$ in. wide and the other by $5\frac{1}{4}$ in. This will give 4 in. clear to each one and sufficient to cover the frame. The bottom ($21\frac{1}{2}$ in. by 9 in.) may be cut last. Use the thinnest part of the hide

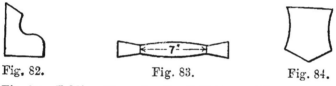

Fig. 82.   Fig. 83.   Fig. 84.

Fig. 82.—Folding Paper for Small Pattern. Fig. 83.—Part of Bag Handle. Fig. 84.—Tab.

for welts, cutting strips for this purpose $\frac{1}{2}$ in. wide and as long as they can be got. Join together into one length by paring the ends with a knife and making a short lap with glue or paste.

A pattern for the tab by whose means the bag is pulled open is shown by Fig. 84.

Make a few four-cord threads of brown hemp, fasten in a pair of the smaller needles, and choose an awl of suitable size. Take one of the bands and one side-piece, lay them face to face, and start sewing from one bottom corner of the side-piece, placing one end of the band level with it and running the welt between the two. Sew round until the opposite bottom corner is reached, tie the threads over the edge, and sew the other side-piece and band together the same. There will probably be a little to trim off the bands to bring the ends level. Do this, and mark each end 4 in. from the seam ; this should leave on one $1\frac{1}{4}$ in. to cover the small part of the frame, and $2\frac{1}{4}$ in. for the larger.

Next take the bottom and commence sewing from one corner of this and the bottom of the side-piece, running a welt in as before. Continue along the end of the bottom, sewing this to the end of the band until the mark already mentioned is reached, run the welt only to the bottom for $\frac{3}{4}$ in., and then take up the end of the other band at the mark 4 in. from the edge. Continue sewing until the place started from is reached, treating opposite sides and ends exactly alike.

The bag, being inside outwards, must now be turned. Do this by placing the left hand in one corner, and with the other hand forcing the leather

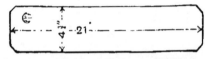

Fig. 85.—Half of Bottom Stiffening.

downwards until it begins to fold over ; then take the other corner of that end, and serve it the same, working both down until they are quite clear. Proceed with the other two corners in a similar way, and the bag will be turned. If enamelled hide is being used, and the weather is cold, warm the leather gently and carefully before turning.

Hammer the corners down from the inside, and press with the hand quite close to the seams all round them ; this will give it a more natural shape to receive the stiffenings. Now take the 2-lb. board, and cut two pieces 21 in. long by $4\frac{1}{4}$ in. wide (Fig. 85). Cut quite $\frac{1}{4}$ in. off each corner to allow them to fit close up to the seams, and try them in before gluing. The proper method is to bend up the stiffening-piece in the centre, put one end in first, then the other end, and finally press down the centre ; this stretches the leather to its full length, and makes a solid bottom to the bag. When satisfied that it is a good fit, glue one piece, place it inside, rub well all over with the rubbing-bone, and glue in the other half. There should be a space of $\frac{1}{4}$ in. between these from end to end.

Stand it on one side for an hour or so for the glue to set properly, and, while waiting for this, cut out the stiffenings for the sides and make the handle. The stiffenings for the sides will need to be $\frac{1}{4}$ in. smaller all round than the leather, or perhaps more if the leather is very stout or the seams are too great a distance from the edges. Cut off the lower corners the same as the bottom stiffenings. Try them in before gluing, remembering that these also must fit very tightly. Use the bone freely all over, so that no part is left untouched, or there will be blisters where the glue does not adhere to the leather. Use the glue quite hot, see that it is not too stiff, and get them into position as quickly as possible.

When preparing the glue, it is a good plan to break it up and soak in cold water for twelve hours ; this, when melted down, will be found to be about right for use.

The stiffening of the bands is purely a matter of fancy ; some like a bag to set out square, whilst others prefer to strap it up close when nearly or quite empty. If it is decided to stiffen these, it must be done after the bag has been framed, using strips from the 8-oz. boards $3\frac{3}{4}$ in. wide.

To make the handle, take a piece of good strap leather 10 in. long by 1 in. wide ; cut to shape as in Fig. 83. Glue together a lot of odd pieces about $6\frac{1}{2}$ in. long by $\frac{1}{2}$ in. wide and the same thickness, and, when dry, pare the edges away until it is perfectly round and slightly tapering towards each end. It is then divided and glued top and bottom to Fig. 83, the ends of this having been previously passed through the handle rings and turned back to form a chape. Put a few stitches through close to the rings, and cover with a piece of cowhide long enough to go through the two rings and along the underside, then stitch it. Trim and dye the edges, rubbing them afterwards with a piece of cloth to produce a polish. It is a good plan to put the plates through the rings before gluing together, as this often proves difficult when made up.

When the stiffenings are firmly set, fix in the bottom nails, and sew on two leather loops for straps (Fig. 86); then proceed to fit in the frame, placing the widest band over the largest half of the frame. Allow the leather to cover the thin iron band and reach half-way down the other part joined

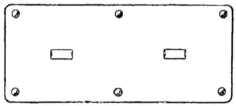

Fig. 86.—Bottom of Gladstone Bag.

to it at right angles. This will leave a good margin inside when sewn through. A hole large enough for the key-barrel of the lock must be cut and passed over it, and another hole the same size cut underneath, continuing this right through to the edge, so that it will fit closely between the under part of the iron band and the lock.

Oblong slots are punched across the iron band of the frame to allow the flexible claws on the fittings to pass through. Take the lock-plate first, and with a fine-pointed knife puncture the leather exactly over these, pass the claws through, and turn them down quite close on to the frame. Then take the handle and fix it.

The strap loops are fitted next; and if slides

have been bought, the leather must be cut away the same size and shape as the slots in the frame before being fixed. In bending down the claws, each pair should be bent inwards, and a piece of leather or similar material laid on anything solid to protect the plated parts whilst being gently hammered down. The shoes should be fixed last; then cut two slits in the narrow band for the lock-catch to pass through.

More expensive frames have solid fittings; these have screws cast on them, and are fitted to the frames by small nuts, round holes being punched to pass the screws through.

It is now ready for sewing. Take the ball of black flax, and make a few five-cord threads, using beeswax for these instead of shoemakers' wax. Cut them in halves, and fix a large needle to one half. The method of sewing in the frame is different to sewing the seams. Commence at one end of the frame, push the awl through, then make another hole in advance of that at a distance equal to the intended length of the stitch. Bring the needle up from the bottom through No. 2, and pass down through No. 1; pull out the full length, make a third hole, bring up the needle, and pass down through No. 2 hole; then up through No. 4, and down No. 3; and so on. This gives an ordinary-looking stitch on the top, but below it has the appearance of a cable, and is called back-stitching. Continue until all the frame is sewn, missing those places where the tie-pieces in the frame are in the way. A tab of leather by which to pull the bag open when in use (Fig. 84) must be sewn on where the lock-catch is fixed to the frame.

The lining must now be cut out. For the sides and bands it is cut the same size as the leather, and the bottom is made in two pieces 22 in. by 6 in. each. This leaves enough stuff to make a strong fold when sewing it with the division board along the centre

F

of the bottom. The covering for the division board
is cut fully 1½ in. deeper than the board. One side
is glued on first, and the pocket flap and strap-
chapes are sewn on before gluing on the other side.
Figs. 79, 80, and 82 show how to cut the pocket and
flaps. For these as well as the bindings a thin roan
or good skiver must be bought. A bright scarlet
looks well, and also wears much better than some
other colours. Strips for binding should be ¾ in.
wide, and carried beyond the bottom of the board
to strengthen it.

A piece of thin strawboard, the same shape as
dotted lines in Fig. 79, must be cut for stiffening the
pocket, and another piece (Fig. 80) for the flap.
Glue these to the leather and a piece of lining over
them ; that for the flap is the full size of the leather,
and of some fancy coloured material. Paste a binding along the top of the pocket, and one round the
flap, or cut the leather sufficiently large to fold over
and form a binding. Fix the pocket and flap in the
centre of the division board, and stitch them round ;
then sew a chape (Fig. 81), with a ⅝-in. buckle and a
loop, on each side, using the single needle and
thread (yellow is best for this purpose) as in sewing
round the frame. Glue the other lining piece over
the back, trim off any inequalities, and paste on
the binding. There are many domestic sewing
machines which are quite powerful enough to sew
through this binding and also the pocket and flap,
and, where one is ready to hand and capable of
doing the work, it should be used. The lining also
may be sewn by a machine.

When this is finished, lay it on one side and paste
in the linings, which should be put in free from
creases and should firmly adhere to the stiffenings.
Pasting well up under the frame enables the lining
to fold neatly over, and makes the work of sewing
it in much easier. Begin to sew in the lining at one
corner near the bottom, using a long needle and

black thread, running the thread under the fold and bringing it through one of the holes previously made in sewing in the frame. Pass it through the next hole, and run the thread under the fold again.

When the lining has been stitched in all round, place the bottom of the division board between the linings at the bottom, fold all surplus stuff inside, and run them together with hidden stitches. Sew two straps 5 in. long by ⅝ in. wide into the two corners of the frame to buckle to the chape pieces, and in the other side of bag sew in four straps, two of which should have buckles. These are sewn

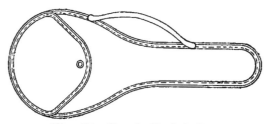

Fig. 87.—Tennis Racket Case.

through the seam, the stitches lying hidden in the welting. The bag is now complete.

It is proposed to give designs and instructions for making four or five different kinds of tennis bags. The making of any of these is not difficult.

Fig. 87 is an illustration of an ordinary tennis racket case, which may be made of a waterproof material, check or twill, or of brown canvas or japanned duck, the edges being bound with leather to give greater strength. A leather handle is fixed on, as illustrated. This may be either a flat strip about ½ in. wide or a strip of thinner leather ¾ in. wide, and rounded by stitching the two edges together, leaving rather more than an inch at each end flat for sewing on to the case.

The front piece is cut square across at the broad end, and a leather binding stitched along it; a leather binding must also be sewn round that part of the flap which opens. Cut the binding for the flap and across the top of the front $\frac{1}{2}$ in. wide, and for the edges $\frac{1}{4}$ in. wider. Paste the flap and front piece at the edges to the back piece, and when dry sew on the binding with a beeswax thread made of fine yellow hemp or flax. It will be found that these waterproof cases preserve to some extent the tension of the strings and help to check the frame from warping.

Fig. 88 shows a tennis bag without any frame, similar to a school satchel, but much larger; it is

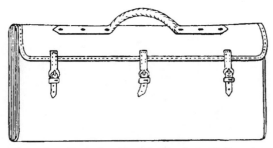

Fig. 88.—Case for Tennis Racket, Balls, etc.

cut in three pieces, one large piece forming the front, back, and flap, and the other two pieces the gussets. Take a piece of waterproof goods 30 in. by 36 in. ; mark off 10 in. for the front, 6 in. for the bottom, another 10 in. for the back, and 6 in. for the top ; this will leave 4 in. for the flap. Each of the two gusset pieces is cut 10 in. by 6 in. Mark one end of the large piece 10 in. from the end on each side, round off two corners, and bind it with a thin strip of leather. This forms the top and flap of the bag. The gussets must be bound along one of the narrow ends ; this will form the top of the gussets.

Before sewing the parts together, three buckles with chapes and loops must be sewn on the front piece about 6 in. from the top edge—one buckle in

the middle and another 3 in. from each edge—and
the straps to meet them may also be sewn on before
the bag is made up or left till the last, as these can
be more easily got at.

To make the handle, take two pieces of leather
14 in. long by 1 in. wide, place a piece of stout cord
or rounded leather between them, about 7 in. long,
and stitch them together far enough to form the
handle proper. This will leave about $3\frac{1}{2}$ in. at each
end to be sewn on to the bag, or it can be fastened
with rivets, as shown in the diagram.

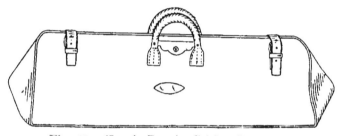

Fig. 89.—Tennis Bag in Cricket Bag style.

These bags, which have the advantage of being
very light to carry and inexpensive to make, may
also be made by sewing the gussets in and running
a welt between the edges, turning the bag afterwards as in making a Gladstone bag. This is not
such a strong way, and necessitates putting in a
lining to hide the rough edges of the seams. The
lining may be a plain one, or fitted with pockets, as
described later.

The exterior of a very popular form of tennis
bag is shown by Fig. 89 ; such a bag, made throughout in cowhide, will last for many years. These
bags are made in various styles, some of brown
waterproof canvas or carpet throughout, others
with leather bottoms only, whilst some have, in
addition, leather gussets ; the most expensive, and,
of course, the most lasting, are made throughout in

cowhide. There is no difference whatever in the method of making these, and the choice of material must be left to individual taste and resource. The bag when closed resembles an ordinary cricketing bag, but is not so long. The frame of an ordinary full size cricketing bag measures 37 in., whereas that of a tennis bag is only 29 in. long. Then, again, the width of the bottom in a bag used for cricket varies from 5 in. to 10 in., but in a tennis bag it seldom exceeds $6\frac{1}{2}$ in.

Fig. 90 is an illustration of the frame used for this kind of bag, and is on the same principle as the ordinary brief-bag frame. The lock-plate and

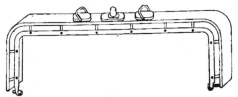

Fig. 90.—Tennis Bag Frame.

handle-rings and plates are shown in position, and are attached to the frame when covered by turning over the metal claws fixed to them on the underside of the frame, or, in the case of solid fittings, by screwing on small nuts.

In measuring for the length of a bag, take the entire length of the frame, and at the same time decide what depth it shall be. It is assumed that the bag is 10 in. deep, 29 in. long, by 6 in. wide. For this obtain a piece of leather $29\frac{1}{2}$ in. by $29\frac{1}{2}$ in., marked off as follows: $2\frac{1}{4}$ in. for covering the large half of frame and $1\frac{1}{4}$ in. for the small half, 10 in. for each side, and 6 in. for the bottom. If the bag is to be made with only the bottom of leather, the pieces for the sides will measure $29\frac{1}{2}$ in. by $11\frac{1}{4}$ in. and $29\frac{1}{2}$ in. by $12\frac{1}{4}$ in. respectively. The gussets will be 10 in. by 6 in. in both cases.

Run a welt of thin leather round in sewing the seams, and as these are sewn on the inside of the bag it must be turned, and in order to make it very firm a piece of stout millboard 29 in. long by 5½ in. wide must be glued and placed in the bottom within the seams, and rubbed well down all over it so that it will hold fast and there are no parts separated.

Special studs are used as a protection to the bottom, and these also assist in keeping the millboard in its place. Eight of these must be fixed in, as shown in Fig. 91, the claws attached to them being opened and turned down on to the stiffening inside. The method of making the handle is described on p. 79.

Place the frame inside the bag, mark and punch

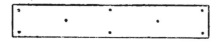

Fig. 91.—Studded Bottom of Tennis Bag.   Fig. 92.—Turn-clip.

a round hole for the key-barrel, fix on the lock-plate and handle-plates, and secure it in position for sewing by a stitch or two at each end near the gusset seams. See that these seams exactly meet when the frame is closed. Begin sewing from one end on the right about 1 in. round the bend, and continue to the left-hand end of frame the same distance round the bend ; then sew in the other half of the frame in the same manner, stitching a tab of leather for pulling the bag open on the opposite side to the one shown in Fig. 89. The two outside straps and buckle pieces must now be stitched on. These should be not less than 8 in. long by 1⅛ in. wide, and of good leather. A name-plate should also be fixed on.

In place of the outside straps a very strong and simple fastener is shown in Fig. 92. This is fixed to the frame in a similar manner to the other fittings. Under the plate which lies along the top of the frame is a spring which acts on the bar, connecting the two sides of the clip, and holds them in any desired position.

The bag is now ready for lining. A good linen, either plain or fancy-striped, is the best for this, and if cut the same size as the outside of the bag, will allow plenty of stuff for strong seams and turning in for stitching to the frame and tops of gussets. It will be noticed that pockets are made on the linings to hold the balls, rackets, boots, etc. When

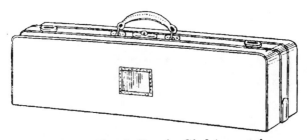

Fig. 93.—Tennis Bag in Gladstone style.

articles of clothing are to be carried in the same bag, it is a good plan to make these pockets of some waterproof material, and large enough to completely envelop the contents, in order to protect the clothing from becoming soiled or damp through getting in close contact with them. Buttons are sewn on the lower parts, and button-holes are cut in the flaps of the pockets, or loops of elastic may be fixed to the latter.

When the lining is finished, place it inside the bag, fold inside all surplus stuff, bend the tops of the gussets inside about 1 in., and sew the lining gussets over and over to these. Then run the thread inside the fold of the lining when stitching the remainder to the frame, bringing the needle to the outside, and making a short stitch in returning it through the frame. The straps to hold tennis bat, etc., can be either riveted or sewn on.

Fig. 93 is a tennis bag made on the Gladstone principle, the only difference being in the depth of the frame and the interior. The lining is fitted with straps and pockets.

A tennis bag made on the half-Gladstone principle is shown by Fig. 94. The frame is fixed to

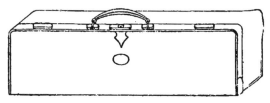

Fig. 94.—Tennis Bag in Half-Gladstone style.

one side of the bag instead of being placed proportionately in the middle. In this case a special frame must be made, and in ordering the frame it must be specified that it is required for a bag of this description.

It will be an easy matter for anyone to make a cricketing bag from these instructions by getting a suitable frame, and making due allowance for the increased dimensions in cutting out the bag.

CHAPTER VIII.

PORTMANTEAUX AND TRAVELLING TRUNKS.

PORTMANTEAUX are expensive things to purchase but not difficult to make, and in this chapter full instructions will be given for making two of the most popular and useful kinds.

Fig. 95 illustrates an "Imperial" trunk, which is of the same shape as a box, and has a flanged lid to keep out the wet. Fig. 96, p. 93, is a sketch of a "Railway" trunk, also called a "folding" trunk.

Frames, material, and all necessary fittings must be purchased. Good japanned canvas, black or brown, 7 in. wide, costs 2s. per yard ; and 2 yds. will be required for a 30-in. "Imperial" of the dimensions given in Fig. 95. The other requirements will be a frame, 6d. ; 4 yds. of 1-in. iron band for strengthening the lid, about 4d. ; $\frac{1}{2}$ lb. of large, round-headed, copper rivets with washers, 8d. ; $\frac{1}{4}$ lb. of $\frac{3}{8}$-in. and $\frac{1}{2}$-in. flat-headed copper rivets and washers mixed, 4d. ; two pairs of brass handle loops, 8d. ; two 1$\frac{1}{2}$-in. brass roller buckles, and one 1-in. ditto, 5d. ; a lock, from 6d. to 2s. 6d. according to quality ; a pair of battens, 6d. ; 3 yds. of striped lining (best, 6d. per yard) ; a welting belly for binding the edges, 10d. per lb.—about 1s. to 1s. 3d. ; and a basil, about 1s. The handles c may be bought ready-made for 9d. each ; but if it is decided to make these, the leather, and also that for the straps and chapes, strap-guides B B, and lock cover A, had better be bought of a saddler, who will cut them to the necessary size. This leather will cost about 3s. Procure also two strawboards 30 in. by 54 in., 6d. each ; 1 lb. of good glue, 6d. ; two or three awls, 4d. each ; a packet of No. 2 harness needles, 2$\frac{1}{2}$d. ; a glue-pot and brush ; and a ball each of hemp and wax.

Begin by cutting the stiffenings to the required size:—16 + 16 + $15\frac{1}{2}$ = $47\frac{1}{2}$ in. by $29\frac{1}{2}$ in. for the body of the trunk. See that the ends are perfectly square, then mark each side the distance mentioned ; lay a long straight-edged rule across, and " score " the board. " Scoring " is cutting the board half-way through its substance, so that when it is bent to form the bottom the front and back rise freely to the proper shape, and the bottom lines will be true

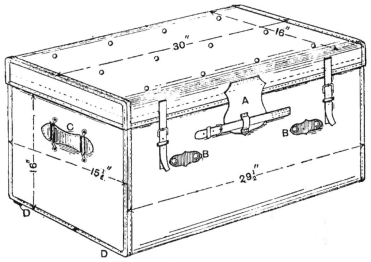

Fig. 95.—Imperial Trunk.

from one end to the other. Next cut the boards for the ends—16 in. by $15\frac{1}{2}$ in. each. The bottom corners are slightly rounded.

The flange of the lid is to be 3 in. all round, so cut a board 30 in. by 22 in. and score it 3 in. from each narrow side. The flange pieces for the ends of the lid are cut separate from this and measure 16 in. by 3 in. each. Next cut the canvas. Lay this japanned side down, place the stiffenings on it, and mark them round, leaving a little surplus from the edges of all the patterns. Do not be too sparing in cutting.

Having cut out the canvas, the next thing will be to glue it to the stiffening. Use hot glue, work the brush rapidly, and be smart in uniting the parts together. Glue the inner surface of the canvas first, then the stiffening board, taking care that the glue is put on to that side of the board which has been scored, or it will not bend properly. Place the board in position on the canvas and rub it well all over until the two adhere together in every part. Glue the canvas and stiffening of the lid together, scored lines to canvas ; then treat the trunk ends, and finally the flange ends, of the lid in the same manner. Weights should be placed on any parts which show a tendency to rise, but do not disturb any portion until the glue is well set.

The edges may then be trimmed with a sharp knife, leaving the canvas perfectly even with the board. That part of the lid which forms the front of the flange must have a basil leather lining pasted along the inside, and a binding of the same leather along the edge. The flange ends are treated in the same way. Cut the lining 30 in. long by 2 in. wide for the front, and 16 in. long by the same width for each flange end. Paste these on first, and bind the edge of each with a strip of basil 1 in. wide. Fold and hammer this down before pasting it so that it will set better, the under part being rather wider than the top ; there will then be no fear of missing any part in the stitching process.

Patterns for the handles, the lock cover, and strap-guides should be cut out of stout paper. Fig. 97 shows a finished handle ready for fixing to the trunk ; it is 11 in. long, $2\frac{1}{4}$ in. full width, $1\frac{1}{4}$ in. where the brass handle loops will cover, and $1\frac{1}{2}$ in. in the centre. The brass loops are $\frac{1}{2}$ in. wide, so, by cutting the spaces 1 in. long, the handle slides and becomes full when in use, and will lie level on the trunk ends when released.

To make a pattern for the handles, fold a piece

of paper 11 in. long and mark it 1¼ in. from the
folded edge. Double the paper so that the line is
at top and bottom; prick it through ⅝ in. from the
edge where the spaces for the metal loops are
shown, and ¾ in. at the fold in the centre. Fashion
the shape of the handle by marking a curved line
between this and the point, and cut out with a pair
of sharp scissors. The pattern will then be similar
to Fig. 98 without the loop spaces removed, as
shown by dotted lines. A pattern for the lock

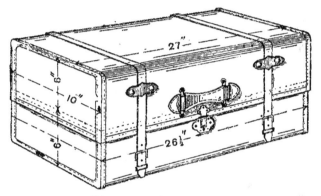

Fig. 96.---Railway Trunk.

cover, 7 in. by 6 in., and one for the strap-guides,
4 in. by 2 in., can be worked out from these instructions.

To cut out the handle, take two pieces of leather
11 in. by 2¼ in., lay the pattern on each, and mark
it round and cut out, but do not remove the loop
spaces. These two pieces form the tops of the
handles. With a pair of compasses mark them
round ⅛ in. from the edge, then fix a bottom piece
to each with two nails (one at each end) and stitch
them together. Shave the edges with a spokeshave, rounding them at that part where they are
gripped.

Next cut out the spaces for the loops, using an

ordinary carpenter's chisel 1 in. wide. Hold the chisel erect and drive it through with a mallet. To rivet the handles on the trunk ends, lay them in position about 4 in. from the top; see that there is the same space at each of their ends, place the brass loops over so that each one touches the points nearest the middle of the handle, make holes through the canvas, and pass up the rivets from the inside. Lay the heads of the rivets on a solid iron and burr the points well on to the metal loops.

The flange ends and front may now be stitched. Sew the binding first with a three-cord thread, about four stitches to the inch. From the binding, mark each piece 1¼ in. for the second row of stitching. This holds the other edge of the lining piece. Cut off a piece of iron band 62 in. long, and slide this within the leather lining on the front, leaving 16 in. of band at each end. Bend these at right angles, then slide each into one of the flange ends. By bending down the back part of the lid, this is brought to the required shape. The end pieces should lie just inside the other part, and should be held in position by being coarsely stitched over the edges.

Prepare the body of the trunk in a similar manner. The ends are placed just within the edges of the other part, and coarsely stitched over in the same manner as the lid. Do not make the stitches too deep, or the binding will not hide them. Put the frame into the top of the body; it must be inside, and level with the top all round. It is fixed by stitching a strip of basil leather round the frame and over the edge of the body. The basil will set better if slightly wetted first.

The outside bindings should next be cut; these are taken from the welting belly, which is a piece of ox-hide specially dressed for this class of work. Cut sufficient strips to go round each end of the trunk; by paring the ends of each strip and lapping

them about $\frac{1}{2}$ in. the required length—about 12 ft.—
may be made. Use a little glue for sticking the
strips together. For the stitching, mark it on each
side about $\frac{1}{16}$ in. from the edge with a pair of compasses. Begin by binding the body of the trunk
first, then the lid. The binding must cover all the
stitching previously made in basting the parts
together, and should be folded over the edge so
that an equal portion of it is on each side. Proceed next to fix the buckle chapes, strap-guides,
and lock.

The lock is first let in by cutting away the
material so that the plate rests on the canvas, but
the case of the lock passes through. A narrow strip

Fig. 97.—Trunk Handle.

of stout leather is placed under the plate at the top
so that the hasp, which is riveted to the lid, may
enter it freely. The lock plate at the bottom is
riveted down close to the canvas, the rivets being
passed through from the inside of the trunk and
burred over on to the plate.

Guides B B for long straps are now fixed, large
round-headed rivets being used for these. Washers
are placed on the rivets on the inside before they
are burred over. The buckle chapes for the short
straps on the lid are stitched on, and a 1-in. buckle
and strap sewn on for holding down the lock cover.
Battens D D are fixed to the bottom with nails or
screws. Small rollers let into these battens provide a means for easily shifting the trunk.

To strengthen the lid, it is necessary to affix
strips of iron band, the position of which is denoted
by the four rows of rivets (three in each row) shown
by Fig. 95. Cut four pieces of the iron band $18\frac{1}{2}$ in.

long, and bend them at right angles $2\frac{3}{4}$ in. from one end, so that they may strengthen the back of the lid. Punch a hole in each of these ends, also three holes in the other parts to receive the rivets. Before fixing these, it will be necessary to stitch the hinge-piece to the back of the lid. This must be of good pliable leather, 30 in. long by 2 in. wide. Fix it on to the lid so that half is left clear for stitching to the body. Lay the iron strips inside the lid, and fix them by twelve round-headed rivets as shown. Rivet the bent ends to the back of the lid with $\frac{1}{2}$-in. flat-headed rivets, passing them through the hinge-piece from the outside.

Place the lid on the body to find the exact places for the hasp and the short straps. Mark these distinctly, rivet the hasp, and stitch on the straps, after which the lock cover may be stitched on. Line both the lid and the body before connecting them, as they will be less cumbrous to manage in two parts. Thin the glue for this work; the better the quality of the lining the less chance has the glue to show through it. Cut the lining to the sizes required, and see that all the stripes are in one direction. The end pieces should be cut large enough to lap a little way on to the other parts. Leave a part of the back lining in the body not glued down, so that in sewing the lid on the stitches are covered by it.

The lid and body are now ready for joining together. Place the lid on evenly, then secure the hinge-piece to the body of the trunk by nails at intervals along it. Drive in at least a dozen nails, then stand the trunk on one end. Pull open the lid a little, commence stitching the hinge-piece from one end, and continue as far as can be reached. Turn the trunk over and sew from the other end until the stitching meets. Glue and fix the part of the lining which was left, fix two pieces of web to stay the lid when open, and the trunk will be finished.

Although the "Railway" trunk (Fig. 96, p. 93) is different in design, the foregoing instructions will apply generally to the method of making it. The dimensions shown are the proportions of an ordinary 27-in., the largest size conveniently carried by one handle, which is placed near the lock. A pair of frames is required for a portmanteau of this shape, these being known as the body frame and the top frame. In the best quality, the sizes of iron used for these are:—For the body, $\frac{5}{16}$ in. square, and for the top, $\frac{1}{2}$ in. by $\frac{3}{16}$ in.

The material required for a 27-in. portmanteau of this shape would be:—Canvas, 1 yd.; lining, 2 yds.; basil and welting belly as before mentioned, one lock, one pair of handle-plates, a few rivets of each kind, two 1½-in. buckles, a piece of ¾-in. leather for the handle, two long straps and guides, lock flap and strap to fasten it, a strip of good leather, 27 in. by 2 in., for the hinge-piece, and two stiffening boards as before.

Cut out the stiffening for the top first, 27 in. by 24 in., then for the body, 26½ in. by 23½ in. The end pieces are cut 12 in. by 6 in. for the top, and 11½ in. by 5¾ in. for the body. There is rather more "corner" taken off these end pieces than in the case of the "Imperial" trunk; the stiffening for the body and top must be scored three or four times across, about 6 in. from each end, to allow a more gradual bend.

Glue the canvas and stiffening together, trim the edges, and fix in the end pieces to the body by stitching the edges over and over. The frame for this can now be put in (square iron) and the edges bound according to previous instructions. Cut the basil lining for the top of this portmanteau 3 in. wide, in order that it may cover the top frame in addition to the iron band. Paste this inside, bind these edges with basil, cut off a strip of iron band 50 in. long, run it within the lining on the front,

G

leaving 11½ in. each side, bend these, and pass them along the lining of the two ends. One row of stitching to secure the lining should have been previously made, and the third line marked for stitching in the frame. The first and second rows should be 1¼ in. apart, and the third ⅜ in. from the second.

All the other work is carried out as described for the " Imperial " trunk (Fig. 95), except the division board (Fig. 98), which is made and put in when all the other work is completed. Cut a piece of board 26½ in. by 11½ in., round the top corners a little, and glue lining on to one side. Cut out the pocket

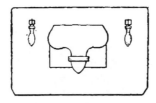

Fig. 98.—Trunk Division Board.

and flap from a piece of thin roan ; the pocket will measure 11 in. by 6 in., and the flap 7½ in. by 6 in. Glue a piece of stout brown paper, 7 in. by 5½ in., to the pocket, leaving 2 in. each side pliable for the gussets. Fold and crease these, and turn the top edge of the pocket in a little to bind and strengthen it.

A pattern must be cut for the flap. Stiffen the flap with stout paper, and turn the edge under all round, using good glue for this. Line both with a piece of coloured cloth, fix them on the lined side of the board, and stitch round. The flap may be held down by a piece of elastic and button, or by inserting a loop as shown.

The buckle chapes on each side of the pocket must next be sewn on, then the other side of the board is lined. The edges, except the bottom, are trimmed, and a narrow binding cut from the same coloured roan is pasted on and stitched round. The lining should extend below the bottom of the board, and it is by this that it is secured to the portmanteau. Fold the raw edges inside and stitch them at intervals along the bottom, passing the thread between the two frames and through the hinge-piece outside

CHAPTER IX.

KNAPSACKS AND SATCHELS.

THE directions about to be given are for making a knapsack measuring 11 in. wide, 9 in. high, and $3\frac{1}{4}$ in. thick; but by increasing or diminishing the dimensions given, of course any other suitable size can be similarly made.

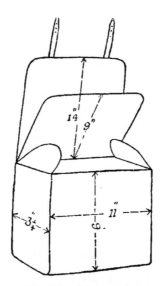

Fig. 99.—Knapsack.

The outside covering of the knapsack shown by Fig. 99 is of rubber-proofed cotton cloth, in purchasing which it is as well to state what the material is for, as a thin stuff is requisite with both sides unglazed. The waterproof material keeps rain from the contents of the knapsack, and prevents any food carried from getting dry. Select a light-coloured material in preference to a dark one, because the sun's heat is reflected by the former and absorbed by the latter, and food is never improved by subjection to an invited temperature of 80° or 90°, quite possible on a summer-day's tramp.

For a temporary knapsack, it has been suggested that calico or holland can be waterproofed by being stretched, the edges being held by tacks, on a flat table, and then rubbed over with a lump of beeswax till it gets yellowish. A warm flat-iron passed over the unwaxed side then causes the wax to saturate the stuff, and this renders it water-

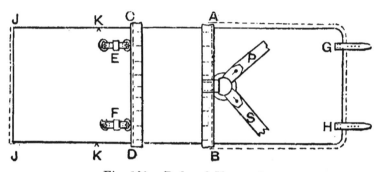

Fig. 100.—Body of Knapsack

proof for some time. It is better, however, to use rubber waterproof.

For lining, some common, white, twilled calico, obtainable at any draper's, can be used.

The necessary leather will be 45 in. of thin, glazed, piping leather 1 in. wide; straps will have to be cut out of strap leather, and buckles for them will have to be bought.

The following are the sizes of the pieces required:—*a.* Two pieces measuring 12½ in. by 1¼ in. (A B and C D, Fig. 100). *b.* One piece measuring 4 in. by 1¼ in. (Fig. 101). *c.* Two pieces measuring 27 in. by 1 in. (P and S, Fig. 100). *d.* Two pieces measuring 7 in. by ⅝ in. (E and F, Fig. 100). *e.* Two

pieces measuring 4 in. by $\frac{5}{8}$ in. (G and H, Fig. 100).
f. One piece measuring 3 in. by $\frac{5}{8}$ in. (s, Fig. 102).
Pieces *c* will have to be reduced in width to $\frac{5}{8}$ in.
at one end for half their length.

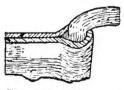

Fig. 101.—Ring and
Holder.

Fig. 102.—Section of Buckle
Leather and Sheath.

Four buckles will be wanted for the $\frac{5}{8}$-in. straps;
two brass studs (Fig. 103), like shirt studs, but
stronger; and a ring $1\frac{3}{4}$ in. diameter (Fig. 104) of
$\frac{1}{4}$-in. round brass or galvanised iron, flattened for
about one-third of its circumference.

Six pieces of cane will be needed, 8 in. long and
about $\frac{3}{8}$ in. diameter. Get also 4 yds. of grey
binding-tape $\frac{1}{2}$ in. wide, some sewing-thread and
needles, and some twist and a piercing-awl for
sewing through the leather portions. The binding

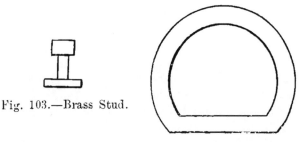

Fig. 103.—Brass Stud.

Fig. 104.—**D**-ring.

can be sewn on by machine, but the rest of the
stitching is done by hand.

From the waterproof cloth and the lining cut
out pieces of the following dimensions:—One piece

measuring 36 in. by 12½ in. (outline of Fig. 100).
One piece measuring 12½ in. by 9½ in. Two pieces
measuring 12½ in. by 4½ in. (outline of Fig. 105).

The lining is pasted to the waterproof cloth and
is left to dry flat under pressure.

From some cardboard ⅓ in. thick cut out two
pieces, each 9 in. by 3¼ in., for stiffening the ends of
the knapsack. Paste them between the 12½ in.
by 4¼-in. pieces (T, Fig. 105). The card must be
central, so that there is a margin of ⅝ in. round

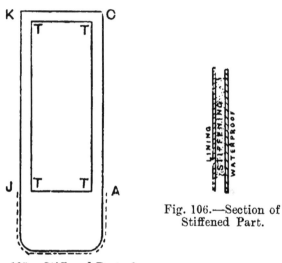

Fig. 105.—Stiffened Part of
Knapsack.

Fig. 106.—Section of
Stiffened Part.

three sides and a margin of 2⅞ in. to the fourth side.
Where the stuffs overlap the card they can be
pasted together, but the whole must be kept flat.
Draw a straight line with lead pencil round the
edges that have the ⅝-in. margin, making the line
⅛ in. from the edge ; then draw a similar line $\frac{3}{32}$ in.
further in—that is, $\frac{7}{32}$ in. from the edge. These
lines (not shown in Fig. 105) are to act as guides
for the seaming, and should be marked on the
lining side.

Round off the corners of the parts shown in Figs. 100 and 105 where indicated, at one end only. A teacup inverted can be used to guide a pencil in marking the part-circle on the lining; a pair of scissors will then cut it out true.

Fig. 106 is an enlarged section of part of Fig. 105, and shows the arrangement of the stiffening card, the waterproof covering, and the calico lining.

Next the binding has to be sewn on. The parts where it goes are indicated in Figs. 100 and 105 by a dotted line outside the outlines. At some places binding is not necessary.

The leather and straps now have to be sewn on. The two pieces $12\frac{1}{2}$ in. by $1\frac{1}{4}$ in. are to be sewn on the 12-in. by 36-in. pieces with twist and the awl, the stitches being $\frac{3}{16}$ in. apart. Fig. 100 shows where the leather goes, and to ensure the correct position it is best to draw two pencil lines across at A B, 14 in. from the round-cornered end, and at C D, 23 in. from the round-cornered end. The seams are to be not quite $\frac{1}{8}$ in. from the edge, and the holes through the leather should be made first, before beginning to sew it to the stuff. These pieces are sewn to the outside of the stuff, and the seamed edges are shown by the dotted lines in Fig. 100.

Only one long edge is stitched; the other is made into six pockets that receive the ends of the 8-in. canes. To form the pockets, eight rows of stitches are made, three stitches in each row, across the width of the leather strip and near its free long edge; the stitches pass through, and further secure the leather to the stuff. The awl-holes should be made for these in the leather at the same time as those for the edge seams. The seam, A B (Fig. 100), besides securing the leather to the 12-in. by 36-in. piece of stuff, also sews the 12-in. by 9-in. piece to it. The lined side of the 12-in. by

36-in. piece goes against the unlined side of the 12-in. by 9-in. piece, and the edge opposite the rounded corners of the 12-in. by 9-in. piece goes along the line A B.

For making the buckle straps skive or bevel the ends of the 7-in. by $\frac{5}{8}$-in. pieces of leather, and, $1\frac{3}{4}$ in. from either end of each, make a hole shaped like an elongated 0, $\frac{3}{8}$ in. long and barely $\frac{1}{8}$ in. wide. The ends of this hole and the holes for the buckle tongues will have to be made by punching out a circular piece with a cutting punch that takes it out clean. The punch can be bought cheaply, but a short piece of steel or brass tubing with the edges at one end ground sharp will make an efficient substitute.

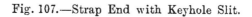

Fig. 107.—Strap End with Keyhole Slit.

Put the buckles on with their tongues through these holes, and bend the skived ends back, as shown in Fig. 102. Put two or three stitches in the skived overlapping ends to hold them together, and with the same stitches sew on a sheath (s, Fig. 102) for the ends of the straps that are to pass through the buckles. The sheath is simply the piece of leather, $\frac{5}{8}$ in. wide and 3 in. long, wrapped once round the middle of the looped strap. It must not be wrapped tightly, or there will not be room for the strap ends to go in; so insert one of these to keep it at the right distance whilst sewing it on. Then sew the looped straps to the outside of the stuff, as shown at E and F (Fig. 100), so that their outer edges are $1\frac{3}{4}$ in. from the edges of the 12-in. by 36-in. piece and their centres are 11 in. from the end that has square corners.

Punch eight buckle-holes in the $\frac{5}{8}$-in. part of the tapering pieces, spacing them equally. In the 1-in.-wide part make keyhole slits (Fig. 107) for the studs to go in. One hole of each pair should be $\frac{1}{2}$ in. from the extremity of the leather, and the other hole $3\frac{1}{4}$ in. from it. The studs passed through these two holes keep the end of the strap wrapped round the $1\frac{3}{4}$-in. ring.

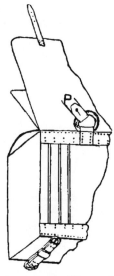

Fig. 108.—Part Back View of Knapsack.

This ring is held to the knapsack by a leather holder made by doubling the 4-in. by $1\frac{1}{4}$-in. piece, and so forming a loop for the flat part of the ring to rest in (see Figs. 100, 101, and 108). The holder is stitched to the middle of the 12-in. by $1\frac{1}{4}$-in. piece, A B (Fig. 100). To the round-cornered end of the 12-in. by 36-in. piece, on the outside, near the end, at G and H (Fig. 100), the two 4-in. by $\frac{5}{8}$-in. pieces of the leather are stitched. They are placed $1\frac{3}{4}$ in. from the 36-in. edge, as in the case of the 7-in. by $\frac{5}{8}$-in. pieces, E and F, for into these they buckle, and so keep the flap of the knapsack down.

Cut the piping leather into two pieces and fold each lengthwise along its centre. Cut a notch $9\frac{1}{2}$ in. from each end so that the folded piping can be bent at right angles there more easily (Fig. 109).

Take one of the stiffened pieces (Fig. 105) and to it sew the piping leather in the following manner: —The edges of the leather are to be close to the edges of the stuff, and the $3\frac{1}{2}$-in. portion between the two notches is to be sewn along the $4\frac{1}{2}$-in. side of Fig. 105, occupying its middle part and leaving

Fig. 109.—Piped Corner of Stiffened Part.

Fig. 110.—Satchel or Cartridge Bag.

a margin of $\frac{1}{2}$ in. at either corner. The other parts of the piping leather—the two $9\frac{1}{2}$-in. ends—are sewn to the two 9-in. sides of the stiffened pieces. Fig. 109 shows a corner of Fig. 105 enlarged, with the piping sewn to it ; the side to which the piping is sewn is the waterproofing, not the lining. The stitches must be $\frac{3}{16}$ in. apart, and along the guide-lines already made $\frac{1}{8}$ in. from the edges. There is no piping between A and J (Fig. 105).

When both pieces have been piped, they are to be sewn to the 36-in. by 12-in. piece (Fig. 100), with a second seam along the second guide-line $\frac{3}{32}$ in. from the first. The relative positions of the 36-in. by 12-in. piece and the two $12\frac{1}{2}$-in. by $4\frac{1}{2}$-in. pieces

are shown by Figs. 100 and 105, where J K C A in one
have to coincide with the same letters in the other,
due allowance being made for the facts that Fig.
100 is drawn to half the scale of Fig. 105, and that

Fig. 111.—Buckle Piece.

on the other side of Fig. 100, J K D B take the place
of J K C A

The seams must be continuous all round the
three sides, and must be made whilst the pieces are
held together, lining outwards. When finished,
the bag must be turned inside out and four fasten-
ing-off stitchings made at the corners A, J, B, and J
(Fig. 100), where these points are sewn to Fig. 105
and its fellow-piece, to prevent tearing. The ends
of the canes must be inserted in their pockets.
Tapes may be sewn to the ends of the unstiffened

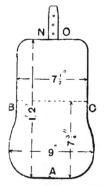

Fig. 112.—Back and Flap of
Satchel.

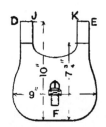

Fig. 113.—Front of Satchel.

parts of the $12\frac{1}{2}$-in. by $4\frac{1}{2}$-in. pieces. Sometimes
one of the straps, P or S, Fig. 100 (whose ends go
into the buckles, E and F), is fitted with a hook-and-
eye attachment to make putting on and taking off

easier than when a buckle has to be undone. In
that case the strap P or S is cut in two about the
middle of the ⅝-in. part, and a brass wire hook is
made and fastened to one end and a brass wire eye
to the other. The buckle is still wanted for adjust-
ment.

This chapter will conclude with a description
of how to make a cartridge bag or satchel. Such a
bag is shown by Fig. 110. To make it, begin by
cutting patterns in paper or cardboard to the
dimensions shown in Figs. 111 to 116. The bag can
be made in cowhide, pigskin, or any other leather
of the same substance and quality, or of canvas
bound with leather. The straps (Figs. 115 and 116),
buckle piece (Fig. 111), and loops, should be made
of brown middling, or solid leather. After this

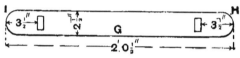

Fig. 114.—Gusset of Satchel.

has been cut to pattern, colour the edges of the
pieces just mentioned with dye to match the
leather, and polish the edges with a greasy rag;
then punch the holes shown in Figs. 115 and 116.

Take the shoulder strap (Fig. 115) and bend the
leather 2 in. from the end and punch or cut a hole
in the centre of the fold for the tongue of the
buckle, which may then be fixed in position. Next
cut a piece of leather, 1⅞ in. by ½ in., and stitch the
two ends together to form a loop; slide this along
the strap to the buckle and sew through the two
thicknesses of strap, starting from L (Fig. 115) on
the one side round to M on the other side. Two
pieces of leather, 1½ in. by ¾ in., may then be sewn
on the gusset or band (Fig. 114) as shown. The
buckle piece (Fig. 111) is made similarly, and afterwards sewn as in Fig. 113, which shows the front.

The short strap (Fig. 116) should be sewn on the
flap (see Fig. 112), the stitching being commenced
$\frac{1}{4}$ in. from the edge and continued for $1\frac{1}{4}$ in. along
each side.   The parts shown by Figs. 112, 113, and
114 should have strong twill lining fixed over the
back of each piece, this being pasted about 1 in.
from the edge.   The front (Fig. 113) should now be
bound with soft leather from J to K, a piece of
leather $\frac{3}{4}$ in. wide being pasted on and marked for
stitching if this is to be done by machine, and
pricked with a pricking iron if hand work is
employed.

The gusset or band (Fig. 114) should now be
welted on the back, a strip of leather $\frac{7}{8}$ in. wide
being folded over and oversewn or tacked about
$\frac{1}{8}$ in. from the edge from H to I (Fig. 114), keeping

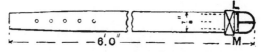

Fig. 115.—Satchel Shoulder Strap.

the two edges of the welting and the edge of the
gusset together.   The back should be folded and
marked at F (Fig. 113); similarly mark Fig. 114 at
G, and bring the two centres F and G together and
tack them strongly.   Also tack together in a
similar way H (Fig. 114) and D (Fig. 113), also I (Fig.
114) and E (Fig. 113).

The whole should now be welted together from
point E to D (Fig. 113), and in doing this, work on
the gusset, having it on top when stitching.   The
piece should next be turned inside out, the face
of the leather being brought outside and the welting being forced out and rubbed with the handle
of a hammer to give it the shape shown at X (Fig.
110).   Next fix the front on the back, joining F
(Fig. 113) to point A (Fig. 112).   Tack the parts
strongly together and bring D (Fig. 113) to B (Fig.

112), and E (Fig. 113) to C (Fig. 112), and tack them. Next oversew or whip the whole together from C (Fig. 112) to B.

The back should next be bound all round with leather from a point under the strap between N and O, overlapping at this point by about ½ in. The binding should be about ⅞ in. wide. Next fold the flap and fasten the short strap to the buckle in front. Run the point of the long strap (Fig. 115) through the loop at X (Fig. 110), passing it round the band or gusset and through the loop on the opposite side.

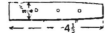

Fig. 116.—Short Strap of Satchel.

The strap should be long enough to pass over the shoulder and buckle, leaving about 6 in. of spare strapping. The parts from D to J (Fig. 113) and K to E should then be turned inward and fastened with six stitches from the inside to the back of Fig. 112. This should be done with an awl and needle, a coarse thread being used.

If brown leather has been employed and has become soiled in handling, wash it with a weak solution of oxalic acid.

CHAPTER X.

LEATHER ORNAMENTATION.

The method of leather ornamentation described in this chapter can be applied to a variety of articles, such as book-covers, blotters, boxes, panels, finger-plates for doors, etc., with fine effect. The tools required are few and can be easily made.

The tracer (Fig. 117) can be made by inserting two pieces of steel knitting-needle in a wooden handle, and filing them to points as shown, one fine and the other blunt. The points should be finished on an oilstone, making them slightly round, so that they do not scratch.

The liner (Fig. 118) is a tool with wheels of different thicknesses, and may be filed up from hard brass, iron, or steel. The edges must be perfectly flat and square, a hole being drilled in the centre for the pin. The shanks to carry the wheels may be of either of the metals mentioned above. A tang is filed at one end for inserting in the handle, the other end being drilled and slotted to receive the wheel and pin. The slot must be just large enough to take the wheel without allowing it to wobble.

The modellers (Figs. 119 and 120) are the shape of the tools used in clay-modelling, and may be of the same material, namely, wood. Box is generally used for the purpose, but any hard wood of close and even grain is suitable. They are easily made with a chisel or knife, file, and sandpaper, the ends being shaped similar to the thumb. Fig. 121 is a view of Fig. 120 from above, showing the ends pointed for working into corners and points of scrolls. The ends of the tool, shown by Fig. 119, are round, and, as seen from above, the larger end is as broad as the middle of the tool ; the other end is slightly smaller. The above tools are all larger at one end than the other, so that the end found most suitable to the line, or work in hand, can be used. All are about 6 in. long.

The grounding-punch (Fig. 122) may be formed

Fig. 117.—Tracer.

from a large French nail, cutting off the head and filing the other or working end to a long blunt point, as shown. It is about 4 in. long. A light hammer completes the list of tools.

The following materials are required :—A slab of slate or marble, about 1 in. thick, to work on— perhaps hard wood would do as well if the surface were planed smooth, sandpapered, and made non-absorbent with a coat or two of varnish ; a bag of sand or sawdust on which to place the marble or wood slab to deaden the noise when grounding ; drawing pins for fixing the design ; a sponge and water for damping the leather ; some bran or fine sawdust and ryeflour for filling the raised parts ; a

Fig. 118.—Liner.

flat ruler, paper, pencil, and compasses. The leather must be thin calf or basil without flaws.

The design has now to be obtained. The companion handbook, "Decorative Designs of All Ages for All Purposes," is invaluable to those who wish to draw their own designs. For transferring the design, with compasses and pencil carefully mark off and draw a number of squares over the

H

original. Then draw a rectangle the full size of
the paper pattern, and divide it into an equal
number of squares. There are now a number of
fixed points, and by noting where the lines of the
design cross the squares, a fair enlarged or reduced
copy can be made.

Fig. 119.—Modeller.

The pattern should be of such a size that a mar-
gin will be left all round, say from $\frac{1}{2}$ in. to $\frac{3}{4}$ in.
according to size. This gives the finished article
a good appearance. The leather, if for a book-
cover, should be cut $\frac{1}{2}$ in. larger all round than this
to allow of skiving and turning over the edge.

Place the leather on the slab, and with the
sponge and clean water damp it carefully and
equally all over. If the leather is wetter at one
spot than another a stain will show; it must be
kept damp throughout the working. The paper
pattern must now be pinned to the leather, and
with the tracer go over all the lines, using con-
siderable pressure, or the pattern will not be trans-
ferred. The ruler should be used to guide the tools
along straight lines.

Fig. 120.—Modeller.

Remove the pattern and go over the lines with
the liner, well pressing it. Any parts to be raised
will now be pressed up from behind, using the
modellers, the depressions thus made being filled
(just filled and no more) with a paste made by
mixing equal parts of fine sawdust or bran and rye-

flour with water. Over these place paper to prevent them sticking where not needed.

The leather is now turned right side up, and the raised parts carefully modelled to shape with the

Fig. 121.—Another View of Modeller.

modellers while the paste is still workable. Then go over the lines again with the liner until they are clear and sharp, and let the leather dry. When quite dry, place the slab on the sand-bag, and, taking the hammer and punch, proceed to stipple

Fig. 122.— Grounding-punch.

or dot in the ground, making the impressions sharp and clear. Much depends on the evenness of the ground. The work is now finished and ready for mounting.

CHAPTER XI.

FOOTBALLS.

FOOTBALLS are composed of two parts—the case, or cover, and the bladder. The case always should be made of leather, and bladders are made from vulcanised sheet rubber of good quality. The shapes most used are the Association (Fig. 123) and the Rugby (Fig. 124).

First of all, it is necessary to decide what kind of leather will be required. The cases are made

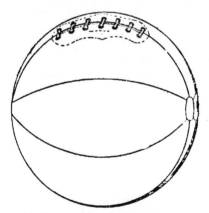

Fig. 123.—Association Football.

from quite a variety of leathers, and many of the cheaper ones are not worth the labour of making up. Much of this leather is manufactured specially for football makers, but good, serviceable cases may be made from leather prepared in the usual way, especially cowhide.

Whole hides vary slightly in size, and cut on the average from twelve to thirteen No. 5 cases ; pieces in various sizes may be bought, and some leather cutters will cut any required size at so much per square foot.

The standard sizes of footballs are as follow:—
Association: No. 1, 20 in. circumference; No. 2, 22 in.; No. 3, 24 in.; No. 4, 26 in.; No. 5, 28 in.; No. 6, 30 in.; and an ordinary match Rugby measures 29¾ in. by 25 in. Other sizes are seldom made except for use in Australia, where they prefer a slightly larger ball, the dimensions of their Rugby match balls being 30½ in. by 26 in.

The case for an ordinary match ball, either Rugby or Association, contains two square feet

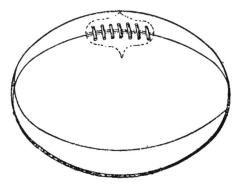

Fig. 124.—Rugby Football.

of leather; but it must not be understood that a case could be cut out of a piece of leather that size. In cutting from small pieces there is more waste than in cutting from a hide. Association cases are mostly made in seven or eight pieces, but some have nine or ten segments, although there is no advantage to be gained in the greater numbers. The easiest to begin upon will be a seven-segment case; the others can be worked out by anyone, as they are all the same size when made up.

For an eight-segment case reduce the width of pattern proportionately, and so with the nine- or ten-segment case. For a No. 5 Association case, made in seven segments, make a pattern 13 in. long by $3\frac{3}{4}$ in. across the middle, as shown in Fig. 125. Take a piece of stout cardboard, and draw on it a straight line 13 in. long; bisect this by a line at right angles, as shown in the diagram. On this line mark off $1\frac{7}{8}$ in. from the centre on each side, and draw segments of a circle through the four points thus obtained. Ordinary compasses or dividers are much too small for this purpose, but there are several methods by which it can be done. One of the easiest is to tie a piece of fine string to a blacklead pencil, hold this in one hand and the string a given distance from it, and draw a line from point to point. Fix the cardboard with a few

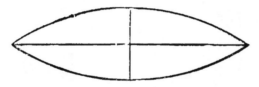

Fig. 125.—Segment of Association Football Case.

drawing-pins or fine nails to the table before marking to prevent it shifting. When the pattern has been cut out, lay it on a large sheet of paper and mark round the pattern seven times on it; this will show how much leather will be required.

In buying the leather, see that the pieces when cut will run in the same direction of the hide as shown in Fig. 126, which shows a hide with pattern laid on, and how it should be cut.

Having cut out the case, mark and cut off each end, if inserted ends are to be put in. These look much neater, and are also stronger, than outside end pieces. Select two segments and place them face to face, then mark one edge of each $2\frac{1}{4}$ in. from the centre; this will leave $4\frac{1}{2}$ in. for the mouth. See that the marks on each are exactly opposite one another. A small piece to line each of these for lace-holes must be cut; this will strengthen them. Mark them as in Fig. 127. The case is now ready for sewing.

The few tools necessary for making footballs are not expensive, and can be bought at any leather-seller's. A knife, a few sewing awls, a No. 3 punch, a ball of fine brown hemp, wax, packet of harness needles, and the usual clamp to hold work whilst

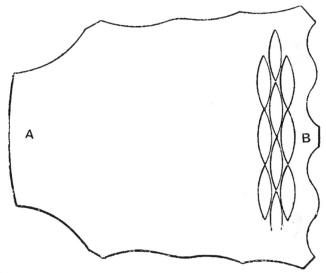

Fig. 126.—Football Pattern Set out on Hide.

being sewn, are all that will be necessary. In-flators may be bought at prices according to pattern and size. Fig. 128 shows the most useful kind; this costs between five and six shillings, its size being 9 in. by 1½ in.

Before beginning to sew the segments together, it will be necessary to make the threads (wax-ends). These may have four strands.

The method of forming a wax-end is as follows: Take the ball of hemp and push the end out from

the centre. The hemp runs out more freely this
way, and the ball will stand perfectly still. A hook
or strong nail must be fixed in some convenient
place, and all being ready, begin by breaking the
end of the hemp to a fine tapering point. This
is done by holding the hemp firmly between the
thumb and forefinger of the left hand, leaving a
few inches hanging down; lay this over the thigh
of the right leg, and with the right hand rub it in
a downward direction, which will cause the twisted
strand to loosen. Then take the end with the right
hand and give it a jerk; the fibres will break, and
the ends of the strands formed in this way, placed
a little distance above one another, will, when
twisted together, give a smooth tapering point.
Stand at a distance of 3 ft. from the hook and begin
to make a thread by holding the end just formed
in the left hand; pass the hemp round the hook
and bring it down with the right hand, and break
off as before. Four strands will make a good
strong thread; carefully examine the points to see
that they taper properly and have no lumps. Rub
the wax up and down quickly a few times, then lay
one point over the right thigh and roll it with the
hand down the leg a few times until it is well
twisted, then repeat with the other point; rub wax
up and down and it is ready for use. Give an additional coat of wax to the points, take a needle,
pass the point of thread through the eye, turn point
of thread back, and twist needle round a few times
to secure it. Fix a needle to the other point in the
same way; select an awl of suitable size, which
should not make a hole larger than necessary, and
all is now ready for sewing.

Begin by stitching on the linings for lace-holes,
which should be large enough to take the sewing all
round the mark. This lining may be held in place
either by being pasted or tacked with two or three
small nails. Place the segment within the mouth

of the clamp, drive the awl through at one of
the points of the pattern marked on it, pass the
needle up through the hole, and draw the thread
through until the middle is reached. This will give
a thread of equal length on each side. Make
another hole with the awl, pass up the bottom
needle as before into the right hand, send the top
needle through to the bottom, and with a needle
in each hand pull through the threads simultane-
ously until they lie on each side of the leather and
form a stitch top and bottom. Sew round until the
place started from is reached, then cut off and sew
the other segment to match. It is assumed that
the case is to have inserted ends, so the ends must
be cut off the seven segments.

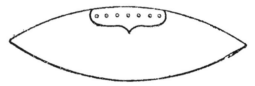

Fig. 127.—Marking Lace-holes on Football Case.

Punch seven holes in each of the two lined
segments for the lace-holes, as shown in Fig. 127.

The case is now ready for seaming. Take two
segments and place them grain upon grain, taking
care that the edges of each are perfectly true.
Place these in the mouth of the clamp, and commence sewing at one end. Be careful to drive the
awl straight through, and as near the edges as may
be without weakening the strong seam; pull both
threads in at the same time and with equal tension; this will give, when finished, a ball of good
shape if the leather has been properly cut. Sew
all the segments together, leaving only the last
seam, where the lace-holes are, unsewn. Be careful to fasten the threads at the ends of each seam
by tying them in a firm knot, or when the case is

turned and inflated the seams will gape open. The last seam should have about two stitches at each end just sufficient to hold them together while the end pieces are being sewn in.

The seams must now be lightly hammered down. The best substitute for a proper iron for this purpose is a small iron foot, such as is used for repairing children's boots on. The smallest size will be large enough, and should be fixed in an iron stand or the usual wooden leg sold for that

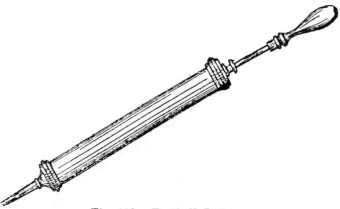

Fig. 128.—Football Inflator.

purpose. Damp the seams well with a wet sponge and push the foot inside the case, taking care that it is always solid where the hammer blows fall. Too much force must not be used with the hammer or the grain may be broken.

When all the seams have been treated in this way, prepare to sew in the end pieces. Take two circular pieces of leather, $1\frac{1}{2}$ in. in diameter, to form the ends; place the case, one end uppermost, between the knees. The hole at each end of the case should be not more than $1\frac{1}{4}$ in. across. Make holes with the awl round the edges before sewing, so as better to guide the worker when sewing the end pieces in ; when sewn hammer down the two seams. The case is now ready for turning. This will be found rather an awkward job, especially if the leather is stout.

The case is the right side out, but this last seam must be sewn inside like all the others ; to do this, drive one end of the case down until it rests upon the other. This will give it the appearance of a large bowl or the half of a huge cocoanut shell. By pulling further apart the half of the open seam which is outside it will be found that the innermost one can be got at. Begin sewing this from the top, and gradually work down towards the laceholes, finishing at the mark showing space to be left for insertion of bladder. Fasten the threads well, as a great strain is on this seam. Place the iron foot inside and hammer the seam ; then push out the case again to its natural shape and drive down the other end, but not so equal as before.

The inserted end piece must rest about half-way along the seam just sewn, and this will bring the unsewn part in the right position for commencing to sew it. About $1\frac{1}{2}$ in. may be sewn, then it will be necessary to shift it a little, and so on until the seam is finished. Lightly hammer the seam while sewing, or it will not shape properly when blown out.

Cut a piece of leather $4\frac{1}{2}$ in. by 3 in. and pare the edges all round to form the tongue-piece. This is stitched on to one of the sides of the opening by half a dozen stitches near the middle hole, and is used as a protecton to the bladder. A hole should be cut in the middle of tongue-piece to allow the pipe attached to the bladder to pass through it.

Now insert the bladder, draw the tube through hole in tongue-piece, lay the tongue evenly inside the mouth, and the ball is ready for inflating. Put the nozzle of inflator into the bladder, and when sufficient air has been pumped in, draw the tube off nozzle, hold tightly with thumb and finger, fold tube over, and tie down firmly with wax-end, taking great care there is no escape of air. Push the tube under the side which is not attached to the tongue, draw the mouth together with a good lace, and the ball is finished.

If the instructions have been carefully followed, a ball, perfect in shape and equal to the roughest wear it may have to endure, will have been produced. With the knowledge already gained, it will be an easy matter to make a ball of any other shape and size. The process is the same, and it only requires some care in calculating for the pattern.

CHAPTER XII.

DYEING LEATHER.

BROADLY speaking, there are two methods of leather dyeing—by dipping, and by brushing.

In the first method, the tanned leather is soaked for a short time in the liquid dye contained in a vat, or it is revolved with the liquor in a closed cylinder. The leather by this means is largely impregnated with the colour. Light-coloured leathers, especially tan colours, are as a rule produced without dyeing ; the tannin liquors are made from materials which yield the required tints, and tanning and dyeing become one operation.

In the second method, a solution of the dye is applied to the surface of the leather whilst spread on a board. This gives a superficial colouring only, the under side of the leather not being coloured. This method is used for applying coal-tar dyes.

If the colour is to be applied by dipping, the preliminary treatment of the leather consists in soaking it in warm water to open the pores and soften the leather, thus allowing it to take up the dye quicker and more evenly. As the skins are often greasy, especially in patches, it may be neces- sary to dip them in a dilute solution of ammonia or washing soda, but this treatment tends to harden the leather and render it harsh, therefore only weak liquors should be employed.

Black colours are produced on leather with salts of iron and galls, etc., or by means of aniline blacks, such as naphthylamine black, indulines, sloelines, etc. For an iron black, the leather is either tanned with gall extract, or, after tanning, it may be steeped for a short time in a bath made of 2 lb. of powdered galls and 1 lb. of logwood chips to 8 gal. of water. This should be rendered slightly alkaline with carbonate of soda or ammonia before use. After steeping in the gall bath, steep it in a solution of ferrous sulphate (green vitriol), 1 lb. to 8 gal. of water, till the black has fully developed.

Aniline blacks soluble in water are not dead-black colours, but have a more or less pronounced violet shade. In order to counteract the effect of this, it is usual to add a yellow dye, such as aniline yellow or orange, or naphthol yellow, in the proportion of, say, one-tenth of the black employed. By using the two dyes combined, it is possible to obtain on leather blacks that are nearly free from violet tint. The blacks mentioned are known as "acid" dyes, and they are readily taken up by leather, especially from a slightly acid solution. Sulphuric acid, however, must not be used, as it causes the leather to rot ; it is better to add a little acetic acid or bisulphate of soda. The amount of dye required varies, but as a rule, 1 lb. to 2 lb. may be taken for 10 gal. of the liquid.

The same blacks may be applied to leather by brushing, which is best done after soaking the leather in water for a short time ; then sponge it with the dye solution, and, after partial drying, another coat may be applied. To get a good black it may be necessary to give several coats, but two coats should suffice if a stronger solution is used.

Other aniline dyes may be applied to leather by dipping or brushing, all that is required being a solution of the dye in water. The amount of dye to be used is best found by experiment on leather scraps, as their staining powers vary.

The aniline dyes may be divided into two classes, "acid" dyes and "basic" dyes. Leather has the greatest affinity for the "basic" dyes, these colours being fixed by the excess of tannin in the hides as tannin-lakes, and if too much tannin is present the leather takes too much colour and becomes over-stained; or it may dye too deeply in patches; thus basic dyes are best employed in rather dilute solutions. Another reason for the use of weak solutions is that basic dyes give a bronze colour if the solution is too strong.

Acid dyes are more suitable for dyeing by immersion than the basic ones, but strong solutions may be applied with a sponge, and will be taken quite readily. Basic dyes are not so suitable for dyeing by immersion unless the excess of tannin is previously removed from the leather by soaking in water. Alkalies must not be used for this purpose, unless afterwards neutralised by dilute acid, as they injure the colour of the dye.

The following is a list of some of the aniline dyes suitable for dyeing leather; it is not, however, a complete list. Compound colours may be made by mixing two dyes

Acid Dyes.	*Basic Dyes.*
Naphthylamine black.	Chrysoidine.
Naphthol blue-black.	Phosphine.
Sloelines.	Bismarck brown.
Nigrosine; water soluble.	Aniline orange.
	Alkali blue.
Acid browns.	Hofmann violet.
Acid green.	Methyl violet.
Naphthol green.	Malachite green.
Fast yellow.	Magenta.

For dyeing leather black by brushing, the leather is stretched and brushed with a strong decoction of logwood. It is then allowed to dry partially, and again treated once or twice with the logwood solution, after which it is brushed or dipped in a solution of sulphate of iron or nitrate of iron. If the black is not fully developed by this treatment the leather is again treated with logwood, or with a solution of quercitron or sumach.

To intensify the black, one of the aniline blacks may be added to the logwood solution. The leather is usually treated with oil during the drying to prevent it getting hard and stiff; it is also worked about for the same purpose.

A solution of shellac in borax is often used to fix the black dye, as that on the surface tends to rub off.

Leather is stained a red colour with one of the aniline dyes, or by first treating it with cochineal extract and tin salts (chloride of tin); the latter, however, is a fugitive colour. The various shades of yellow, orange, tan, red, etc., are also obtained by using solutions of aniline dyes, or by the use of saffron, anatto, fustic, and Brazil wood. A solution of picric acid gives a very pale yellow colour; aniline yellow and phosphine are now largely used for yellow stains. A red dye may be made by heating $\frac{1}{4}$ lb. of Brazil wood (in shavings) with 16 oz. of white vinegar, and then adding a solution of $\frac{1}{2}$ oz. of alum in 4 oz. of water. This is brushed on the leather. A purple dye is obtained from $\frac{1}{4}$ lb. of Brazil wood, 1 oz. of scarlet berries, 16 oz. of water, and $\frac{1}{2}$ oz. of sulphate or chloride of zinc. Adding a little sulphate of copper modifies the colour.

The leather intended for dyeing in bright colours should be as nearly white as possible. Leather that has been tanned, that is, alum-tanned or tanned with pale tan liquors, will be most suitable for the purpose. After dyeing, the leathers are usually finished by smoothing with a "slicker," and drying very slowly, stretching them and working them about from time to time to prevent wrinkling and stiffening. As a finish they may be rubbed with a strong soap solution made with curd or Castile soap. A dull polish may be obtained by using a polishing rag and a little French chalk. In some cases oils and yolk of eggs are employed to aid in softening the leather.

CHAPTER XIII.

MISCELLANEOUS EXAMPLES OF LEATHER WORK.

A NUMBER of miscellaneous articles in leather will have their construction described in this chapter.

Cash bags may be made of soft leather, such as wash-leather or basil. Cut them from 8 in. to 9 in. long and from $4\frac{1}{2}$ in. to $6\frac{1}{2}$ in. wide; have a centre piece to reach to within 2 in. of the top, of the same width as the bag; put the three edges together and tack them, and either backstitch or double-hand them with a fine awl and needles, with linen thread of any colour. Then turn the bag

Fig. 129.—Portsea Purse or Saddler's Purse.

inside out and turn in $\frac{1}{2}$ in. about the mouth, stitching all round the bottom of the turned-down piece. Punch holes $\frac{3}{4}$ in. apart all round the mouth between the stitches and the top, and run a string in and out from each end through these holes so that the string crosses in the holes; knot the ends so that the mouth is closed on pulling the string.

The Portsea purse (Fig. 129) is commonly called a saddler's purse, and may be made easily. The material may be hogskin, light calf, or other light leather of any colour. Cut the back part $5\frac{1}{2}$ in.

I

long, round it at one end for the bottom, leaving
the sides straight ; then round the top, cut the front
piece $3\frac{3}{4}$ in. long, and round it at one end to the
same shape as the back part ; let it be quite square
and straight at the top. Cut the centre piece to
the same shape, and round it at the top.

There are now three pieces ; put these together
and tack them. Having marked the stitches on
the front part, stitch double with beeswaxed linen
thread where the front part begins, and stitch all
round to the opposite side. Then glasspaper the
edges, wet them, and rub with a rag so as to polish
them. Turn down the back part a little above the
line of the front piece, and give the bend a few light
taps with a hammer.

A small button, such as a small front stud, may
be put through the front piece, with a hole opposite
in the overlap to fasten it down ; but this is not
really necessary. If the pocket is made with a
gusset—that is, a piece let in to open it to increase
the capacity—a button will be required to keep it
closed.

For the gusset, cut a thin piece of soft and
pliable hogskin ; it must be long enough to go
round the stitched part of the purse and $1\frac{1}{2}$ in. wide.
Double it down all along the middle, and mark it
along the bent edge with the screw-crease and
prick along the mark ; put in the centre piece of
the purse from the point of the straight end between the two folds of the gusset right up to the
leather at the bend, and turn the gusset so all
round the centre piece, and stitch along the marks
made all round, taking care that with every stitch
the centre piece is caught up. Cut square with the
top of the centre piece on both sides, and tack the
edge of the gusset right opposite on the back and
all round, and stitch the gusset and back together
all the way.

Tack the front piece to the other side of the

gusset and stitch it round; then damp the gusset well, and draw a piece of string tightly against the middle of the gusset between the back and centre pieces; also draw it between the centre and the front piece to pull in the gusset. Put the purse on a flat surface and weight it to keep it flat; leave it so till the gusset dries, and it will then stand and keep its form. Trim and rub the edges, turn down, overlap, and put in the button. Other purses may be made on the principles just described.

It frequently happens—even when a good price is paid for a pair of opera glasses—that the case sold with them soon shows signs of becoming dilapidated. This is owing to the trumpery material these cases are made of, and the slip-shod style of putting them together. The instructions given here are for making a case in solid leather, which, if well-made, will keep in good shape and sound condition for many years. There is no difficulty in making it, the details of construction being soon mastered; and its cost will be but trifling. Brown and patent leathers look and wear well, and both kinds are made up in the same manner.

Fig. 130 gives the three necessary patterns for cutting out an opera-glass case. The body is made of two pieces marked A, which are joined together on each side where the strap goes round. B shows the pattern for the top. A strip of leather $\frac{1}{2}$ in. wide is joined to this and forms the flange. This may be cut in one length and carried right round, or made in two pieces and joined even with the seams on the body. C is the bottom pattern.

Make tracings of the three patterns on suitable paper and paste these to thin cardboard, or sheet zinc of fine gauge. Cut them out correctly, lay the patterns on the leather, and either cut it with a fine-pointed knife round the edge of the pattern, or mark the shape first with a round point and cut out after the pattern is removed.

For colouring the edges of brown leather use a
very weak solution of " size "—1 oz. is enough to
½ pt. of water ; and a few drops of oxalic acid in
solution added to it produces a more brilliant
polish.　If black, or patent, leather is used, colour
the size with a little lampblack or similar pigment.
The edging must be applied hot with a sponge, and
the polish produced by rubbing with a moderately
coarse cloth.

The sling-strap should be 6 ft. long by ⅝ in. wide.
The strap to hold down the lid is 3 in. long by ⅜ in.,
and the four loops to keep the sling-strap in position round the case must be cut 1¾ in. long by ⅜ in.
A number of holes will have to be made in the
straps.

Colour and rub up the edges of straps and loops,
and one edge only on the flange pieces.　Those
edges to be sewn must be finished after the stitching is done.

The buckle chape should be stitched on to the
middle of one half which is to form the body before
the side seams are closed ; it is so much easier to
fix this on to the flat surface.　Mark all parts for
the stitching ⅛ in. from the edges—that is one edge
of each flange piece, the four edges of the body,
and also the top and bottom pieces.

The flange pieces for the body are laid inside
and fixed to the broadest part of each body half.
Secure these in position with a few small nails and
stitch them straight through.　See that the inside
edge is well taken hold of by each stitch, and that
a uniform portion of the flange is in sight.　Having
sewn these on, the sides are now ready for closing
together.　In doing this, the awl must be driven,
not straight through as in the case of stitching on
the flange, but in a slanting direction from the
mark along the surface towards the extreme edge
at the bottom, and then through the other part in
a corresponding manner, bringing the awl out at

the opposite mark. In this manner one edge is made to butt close against the other, and the stitching securely holds them together.

The guide loops for the sling-strap must be stitched on next. Place these evenly across the seams, so that an equal proportion of loop is on either side, and stitch them on, leaving sufficient " slack " to allow the sling-strap to be drawn through. Two small pieces of leather—to form hinges—must also be attached to the body. Stitch the bottom in next. This is put inside the lower

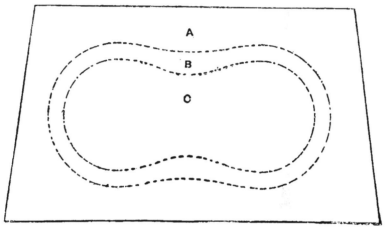

Fig. 130.—Patterns for Parts of Opera Glass Case.

part of the body, the cut edge of this latter being brought flush with the outside of the bottom. Pass the awl through from the mark on the body to that on the bottom—not vice versâ.

The flange piece is next sewn to the lid in a like manner, the cut edge of flange being flush with the outside of the top. Sew this to the two hinge pieces at the back and stitch the small strap to the front. Cut and fit in the baize or velvet lining, using some good paste for fixing it. The case is completed by sewing a buckle and loop into the sling-strap, and passing it through the four guide loops.

Cases for any size of glasses—opera, field, or marine — may be made from these instructions. To get the size of the top and bottom leather, place the glasses on a sheet of paper and take the outside measurement at each end. Then take the length of the glasses, first turning the screw to bring the glasses to the shortest focus, and make some allowance over this measurement for the thickness of leather, etc.

In making a music carrier, such as is illustrated by Fig. 131 below, great skill is not required,

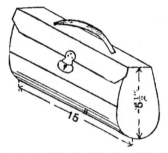

Fig. 131.—Music Carrier Closed.

especially if the instructions about to be given are followed with care.

The shape is of the ordinary round bottom pattern (Fig. 131) so generally used, which possesses the advantage of holding the folded music without any perceptible crease. Fig. 132 shows the lid raised and the front flap dropped ready for receiving the sheets of music as well as for withdrawing them. With this drop flap it is easier to insert and remove the music than would be possible if this portion were united to the ends in the same manner as the back.

The dimensions given will be found suitable for all ordinary sheet music measuring 14 in. by 10 in.,

the case when made up being 15 in. long by 5½ in.
deep. The diagram (Fig. 133) shows how the
various parts are divided, 3½ in. being the drop
flap, 9 in. the bottom and back, 1¾ in. the top of
lid, and 2¼ in. the lid flap. Of course, there is no
necessity to keep precisely to these dimensions,
but they will be found to be very suitable for the
purpose.

Whatever material is used it is essential that it
should be cut in one piece, allowing a sufficient
margin beyond the four edges for turning over—at
least half an inch. Many kinds of material are

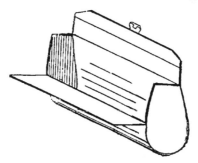

Fig. 132.—Music Carrier Open.

used, from the commonest bookbinders' cloth to
the expensive French moroccos and scented Russia
leather. Common bookbinders' cloth is the
cheapest and the least troublesome to use, but it is
the least durable. Dull-grained American duck
wears better, but is not so easy to work.

Lay the cloth or leather, as the case may be,
face downwards on a level table and proceed to
line out the various parts as in Fig. 133; allow ½ in.
to ⅝ in. beyond when cutting to provide the necessary surplus for folding over the edges. The corners of this surplus must be removed as shown,
so that the edges when folded over the board neatly
butt together. A piece of thin millboard is next

cut 15 in. by 16½ in., the two corners are taken off, and the cross lines scored—that is, cut about half-way through with a pointed knife travelling along a straight edge. This permits the board being folded into divisions without separating the parts. The two lines on each side of the 1¾-in. space are scored, then the board must be turned over and the line for the drop flap (3½-in. space) scored on the other side.

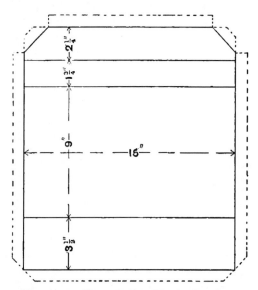

Fig. 133.—Pattern for Music Carrier.

Good bookbinders' paste is next applied to the inside of the material, and the millboard surface is double scored; then lay the board in position on the cloth and press the two firmly together by using the roller (Fig. 134). The pasted edges are next brought over the board and rolled.

The inside lining is cut rather less than the size of the millboard, so that it does not quite reach the extreme edges, but proves sufficient to make a good lap over the turned-in surplus. The rounded ends seen in Figs. 131 and 132 are usually cut from a piece of ¼-in. good deal or mahogany board, and covered to correspond. Place one of these ends in position and fix with an escutcheon pin at the extreme point forming the back, and again just below the drop flap ; then at intervals insert small gimp pins and fix in the other end to match.

The lock and catch are fixed by three pins being riveted through each, and metal handles with bosses and clamps may be bought and easily fixed. When leather handles are used it is a much stronger method to insert the ends through openings made in the top of the case, and then stitch or rivet them ; and it will give a neater appearance if the

Fig. 134.—Hand Roller.

handle and lock are fixed before the inside lining at this part is pasted down.

A leather camera case must be of simple shape, strong, thoroughly waterproof, of a smooth interior, so that it does not scratch the camera, and it should not be heavier than is consistent with durability.

The leather for a camera case is not a very expensive item, and there is little else to add to its cost except the lining and a few buckles and dees, or rings. The patterns may be cut from thin cardboard or brown paper.

For a ½-plate camera case as illustrated by Fig. 135, cut the widest pattern first (see Fig. 136). This forms the outside flap, top, and back of case.

Round the corners well at one end and slightly at
the other, and draw two lines across the pattern,
using a square for this purpose. One line is drawn
across $3\frac{3}{4}$ in. from the end with large rounded
corners—this gives the size of the flap ; and another

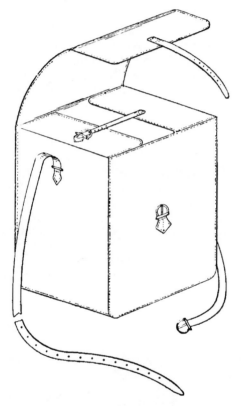

Fig. 135.—Camera Case.

line is drawn 7 in. from this, giving the size of top
and leaving 11 in. for the depth of case, and a total
length of $21\frac{3}{4}$ in. The width throughout is $8\frac{1}{4}$ in.
Next cut a pattern 36 in. long by 7 in. wide for the
gusset (see Fig. 137). The four corners must be
rounded off and lines drawn across the pattern, one

3 in. from each end and two more 11 in. from these. This leaves a space of 8 in. for the bottom. The pattern for the front is a simple rectangle 11 in. long by 8¼ in. wide, two of the corners being slightly rounded.

Black enamelled or brown cowhide is the best

Fig. 136.—Front Flap, Top, and Back of Camera Case.

leather for this purpose, and a camera case this size will take about 3½ square feet. Some pieces of leather for binding the flaps will be wanted; these must be thin and pliable, and cut into strips ¾ in. wide and long enough to reach ½ in. beyond the marks showing the parts to form the flaps. In Fig. 136 the binding starts at A and is continued round to B, as this part forms the top of the case as well as the flap.

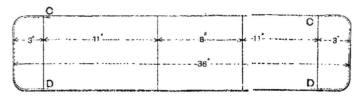

Fig. 137.—Gusset and Flaps of Camera Case.

Leather for the straps and chapes will also be required. For the sling a piece 42 in. long by 1 in., and another piece 14 in. long, same width, for the buckle part. These will be long enough to go twice round the case so that it may be carried in the hand, if desired, the double width of the strap forming a good handle. Chapes for the dees to be fixed to the case must be $3\frac{1}{2}$ in. long and 2 in. wide, cut to the shape of Fig. 138. Those for the buckles are cut the same shape, but only 3 in. long by $1\frac{1}{2}$ in. wide. A hole at x must be cut in these for the buckle. A strap 7 in. long by $\frac{3}{4}$ in. wide for the outside flap, and another $5\frac{1}{2}$ in. long by $\frac{3}{4}$ in. wide for the gusset flaps, and two $\frac{1}{2}$-in. loop pieces, two $\frac{3}{4}$-in. buckles, one 1-in. buckle, and two 1-in. dees or rings, will be all that is required except the lining. This may be either plush, velvet, green baize, cloth, or even thin leather.

With the patterns and materials ready, begin cutting out. Lay the patterns on the leather and see which is the best and most economical way of cutting out the parts, using the stoutest parts for the front and back, as these are subjected to the hardest wear. Cut evenly round the patterns with a sharp knife, running the second finger of the hand holding the knife along the edge of the pattern as a guide, and holding the pattern down firmly with the other hand. Then cut out the lining, one piece to each pattern.

In order that there may be nothing rough inside when the bag is finished, the dee chapes, buckle pieces, and short straps must be sewn on before lining the case. The long straps can be sewn on the dees after the bag is made up. Put the straight part of the dees into their chapes and tack them on to the gussets with two or three small nails to keep them in position whilst being sewn. About $4\frac{1}{2}$ in. from each end will be about the right distance for these, and the shortest narrow strap is sewn on one flap nearer the end and a chape with buckle and loop-piece in on the other. See that these are far enough from the edge to give room for the binding. The chape with buckle and loop must be sewn on the front piece, in about the middle of it, and the other narrow strap sewn on the front flap. The sewing thread should be a four- or five-cord thread of No. 22 hemp.

The leather should now be placed bottom upwards and the lining joined to it by a thin streak of glue or paste round the edges, pressing them well together. If a stiffened case is required, pieces of cardboard cut to the size of the various parts, except the flaps, may be glued between the leather and lining. Trim the lining off level with the leather and paste on the bindings. Before applying the paste to these, fold them over and tap them down with a hammer; this will cause them to go round more evenly and help the paste to unite them to the leather and lining. A three-cord thread of fine closing flax is stout enough for sewing the bindings, and the stitches should be six or eight to the inch.

Before sewing the sides together, place the patterns on the leather and make ink marks on the brown edges of the latter where the lines run across the patterns; this will serve as a guide in fitting the parts together. All the unbound edges must be marked $\frac{1}{8}$ in. from the edge with a pair of compasses to give the lines for straight stitching, and if a saddler's pricking iron can be obtained these lines may be stamped with it and a perfectly even stitch obtained. These pricking irons cost, new, $1\frac{1}{2}$d. a tooth, and are made with teeth ranging from six to the inch to sixteen to the inch, and from three or four teeth to twenty in number. For sewing these seams use a four-cord hemp thread.

If the case is a stiffened one, it will be found rather difficult to sew these side seams in the clamp, but if a box 10 in. by $7\frac{1}{2}$ in. by $6\frac{1}{2}$ in. is made, the case can be tacked on to this and held between the knees whilst being sewn. Stitch the front piece and one edge of the gusset first, and then fix on and sew the back part to the other gusset edge. Shave the edges even with a spokeshave, rub on some dye, and polish them with a soft cloth. It only remains to sew the long straps on to the dees and the case is completed.

The regulations for dog muzzles specify the use of a cage muzzle which shall prevent any possibility of the animal biting, and shall also give perfect freedom in breathing and not hinder the dog from lapping water.

The muzzles sold in shops are generally made to standard sizes, and are only suitable for the dog with an average-shaped head. The sizes given below correspond to those articles, but the method of altering the various parts will be pointed out, so that there will be no difficulty in making a muzzle for any head.

On referring to Fig. 139, the muzzle will be found to consist of four pieces of narrow leather, namely, a nose-piece, the front, the cage proper, and the strap and buckle-piece.

The nose-piece runs from A round the nose and under the buckle at the other end, and has seven slits pierced through it sideways—at A, B, C, D, E, F, and G. Similar slits are cut in the front piece at H, I, and J. In the muzzle or cage-piece, M, O, P, Q, S, there are only two slits at L and N, and in the strap-piece slits are cut at X, R, K, and T.

To make a No. 2 size muzzle—which fits a small fox-terrier dog—cut four strips of leather, each barely $\frac{3}{8}$ in. wide, trim off the sharp edges and rub them up with a rough cloth, first sponging on some warm-coloured size diluted. Make the nose-piece 11 in., front piece 6 in., cage-piece 22 in., and strap-piece 20 in. long. Mark one edge of the nose-piece with a blue lead for the slits, marking first at $\frac{3}{4}$ in. from one end, then at 2 in., $3\frac{1}{2}$ in., and $4\frac{3}{4}$ in. Fold the strap exactly in the middle and mark the edge opposite these, so that the spaces on each side are uniform. There is no necessity to mark one at the other end, as this enters the buckle chape.

Use a sharp, narrow chisel or a penknife for dividing the leather, and be careful to cut it clean through the middle. A gauge, made by nailing some odd pieces of leather on a board, is very useful in firmly holding the leather edgeways for this operation. Having cut the slits, take the front piece and cut a slit $\frac{3}{8}$ in. from each end and one $2\frac{1}{4}$ in. from one end, leaving $3\frac{3}{4}$ in. for the forehead. The cage-piece has two slits only, the first $1\frac{1}{4}$ in. and the other $4\frac{1}{2}$ in., these distances being measured from one end only. In marking the slits in the

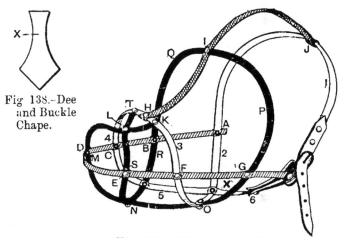

Fig 138.–Dee and Buckle Chape.

Fig. 139.—Humane Dog Muzzle.

strap-piece 1 to 6, start from the buckle end and mark the edge at $2\frac{1}{2}$ in., 4 in., 7 in., 8 in., and $10\frac{1}{2}$ in., and cut the slits. The strap-piece crosses underneath the throat at x.

For fitting the muzzle together, take the front piece, open the slit I, and pass one end of the cage-piece through; fold it to get the slit over the middle, make a hole with a small awl, and drive the nail through to keep it in position. Put a washer over the nail, cut off, and rivet with a small hammer, using a lead piece as a support.

The cage-piece is next passed through the nose-piece at B and G (Fig. 139), and the strap-piece is passed successively through J, A, X, F, H, and C. With the front of the muzzle towards the worker, continue the cage-strip from G through R, D, and K. Then take the other end, and pass it through R, N, E, L, and T. See that all the parts correspond before nailing and riveting.

If possible, try the muzzle on the dog to ensure the various spaces being well apportioned. On small muzzles it is usual to cut a strap 4 in. long by $\frac{1}{2}$ in. wide, and rivet or stitch it to that end of the strap-piece which slides through J. Punch

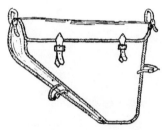

Fig. 140.—Cycle Valise.

four or five holes in it for adjusting to the size of the dog's neck. A chape with double buckle is riveted to the other end.

The lengths of the various parts for muzzles numbered in lists as No. 4, No. 6, or No. 8 size are as follow, the spaces being in proportion to the one illustrated here:

	No. 4.	No. 6.	No. 8.
	in.	in.	in.
Nose-piece	$12\frac{1}{2}$	$15\frac{1}{2}$	20
Front...	7	$8\frac{1}{4}$	$9\frac{1}{2}$
Cage-piece	26	32	40
Strap-piece	23	27	32

For a pug dog, the front and nose-pieces must

be shorter, and the other two parts longer ; the distance H to J (Fig. 139) is extremely short, and the cross at the throat is close to N. For a dog with a long thin head the opposite treatment is necessary. These muzzles have the appearance of being very complicated, but, by following the instructions, it will be an easy matter to make them.

A cycle valise should be light, strong, rainproof, and as commodious as the frame of the machine will permit. Leather or waterproof canvas will answer well for the purpose, and, by making the valise as shown by Fig. 140, it will have sufficient capacity, without being too large or cumbersome. The sizes given will be suitable for nearly all

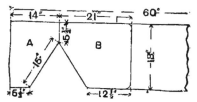

Fig. 141.—Pattern for Cycle Valise.

frames, but where this is not the case the necessary alterations can be made before cutting out the material. To get the correct size of valise, place a sheet of strawboard on one side of the cycle frame, and mark it by running a lead pencil round the inside of the frame. Another plan is to cut out a pattern of the small half from the dimensions given in Fig. 141.

Half a yard of material will be required to make the valise ; the gusset, however, will not be all in one piece, but must be cut from the surplus and joined. If it is desired to have the gusset without a join, ¾ yd. must be bought. This would be most economical if two carriers are to be made, and as the material is suitable for cutting either crosswise or lengthwise, the patterns may be reversed and

J

there will be less waste. Be careful to mark the patterns A or B distinctly, and, in cutting the material, see that the letters are uppermost, or the parts will not be in pairs. In Fig. 141, A denotes the small half, and B the large half with flap.

The gusset is cut 3 in. wide by 40 in. long. Strips of soft hide bellies must be cut 1 in. wide, the ends pared down and spliced together with good paste: about 12 ft. will be wanted. Bind the flap first, then the top of the small half which is to go under it, and each end of the gusset-piece. The parts

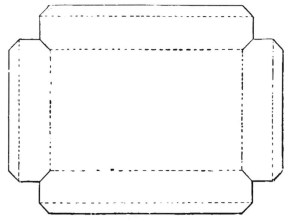

Fig. 142.—Pattern for Leather Covering of Workbox

are then pasted together and bound with leather. The straps for the flap are cut 6 in. long by $\frac{3}{4}$ in. wide, and those for fastening to the frame 10 in. by $\frac{3}{4}$ in. The buckle is sewn into one end of these, and they are stitched on the carrier close to this stitching. To make the sides very firm, stiffen them with pieces of cardboard; the gusset should be kept flexible.

A lady's workbox can be covered with leather in the following way. For the lid or top, measure from the front opening at the lock to the hinge line, and again over the top from each side open-

ing. The inner row of dotted lines in Fig. 142
shows the plan of top of lid; the outer row shows
where it turns over the lower edge; the part beyond this is brought to the under part of frame
resting on the other half of the box. Make a brown
paper pattern and put this on first, to see if it is
correct. The corners, as shown in Fig. 142, allow
for lapping over, which is much stronger and neater
than butt joints. They must be pared down, so

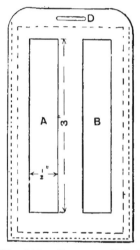

Fig. 143.—Luggage Label.

that the thickness of the lap is not greater than any
other part.

To cover the lower half of the box, take the
outside measurement of the four sides, and cut a
strip of leather 1 in. wider and $\frac{1}{2}$ in. longer; this
allows for turning over the upper and lower edges,
and making a lap joint, which should be at one
of the back corners. Pare down all edges which
are made to lap over and form joints.

For the workbox bottom, cut a piece $\frac{1}{8}$ in. less
than the bottom of the box, and fix this on to cover
evenly the turned edges. Apply a thin coat of glue

to both leather and wood, and press them together. Do the work in sections, thus—the top of the lid first, then the four sides, and, lastly, the turned

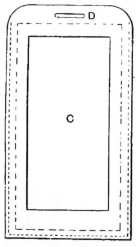

F.g. 144.—Another Luggage Label.

edges at the bottom. The metal hinges should be removed, so that the lid is quite detached from tne lower half of the workbox. If the box is veneered,

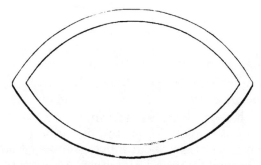

Fig. 145.—Segment of Cricket Ball Covering.

the veneer will have to be well sand-papered, in order to get the glue to adhere properly.

Luggage labels ean easily be made from leather,

which should be stiff rather than soft and oily. To make one of the shape illustrated by Fig. 143, cut two pieces of leather about 4 in. by 2¼ in. and round them off on the top edges. With the back of a knife-blade and straightedge, mark and cut out the pieces A and B, and place them together, with the flesh sides touching ; sew them together

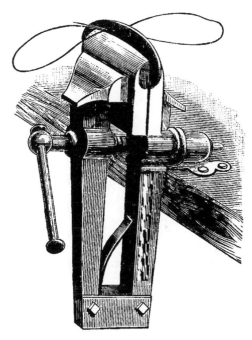

Fig. 146.—Sewing Cricket Ball Covering.

on the three edges, as shown. Cut the slit D through both, about $\frac{1}{16}$ in. to ⅛ in. wide by ⅝ in. or ¾ in. long. A strap about 3 in. long, to be fastened to the parcel, is put through the slit. Thin cardboards (plain postcards are just the thing) are cut to size to slip in the label, when the required name and address, etc., have been written on.

Fig. 144 shows another label, the only difference

being that the front part has a larger space for a full address. The edges of the label can be made glossy and smooth simply by rubbing with a piece of hard wood, bone, or other hard substance, the edges of the leather being wetted.

A cricket ball that will withstand a lot of hard wear may be made from some old corks and some leather. Cut the corks square and glue them to-

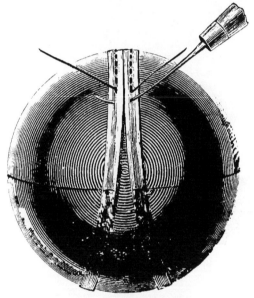

Fig. 147. - Sewing Halves of Covering on Cricket Ball.

gether, and, when they are dry, trim them to an approximately spherical shape. Bind the cork ball round and round with twine until it is of the desired size minus the leather cover. The finished ball should be $2\frac{1}{2}$ in. in diameter.

The leather used for the covering must be strong but not thick. Four pieces to the shape shown by Fig. 145 must be cut, each being half the circumference long and a quarter the circumference wide, and allowing $\frac{1}{4}$ in. all round for the seam.

Soften the leather by soaking it in water for a
short time, and then put two pieces together and
hold them in the jaws of a vice between two pieces
of wood shaped to correspond with the leather (see

Fig. 148.—Section of Sewn Edges of Ball Covering.

Fig. 146). The actual inside of the leather should
be made the outside. The sewing is commenced
with a waxed thread having a harness-maker's
needle on each end ; holes for the needles to pass
through are made with a fine stabbing awl. The
two halves of the cover are made separately, and
when opened the seams are hammered flat.

Then the covers are placed over the twine-and-

Fig. 149.—Holding Cricket Ball during Sewing.

cork ball and the edges sewn together. One way
of doing this is to use a straight awl, cut the edges
off close, and then hammer well to shape. Another
method, more difficult but producing a stronger

job, is to use a slightly bent awl, have the seam
bent over, and then stitch through the four
thicknesses of leather. The latter method is illustrated by Figs. 147 and 148, the latter figure being
a section of the doubled-over leather. Pull the
stitches up tight ; as the leather dries, it will shrink
and become tighter. Having trimmed the seam
with a sharp knife, taking care not to cut the
stitches, flatten the seam by hammering.

The ball may be held whilst sewing by the appliance shown by Fig. 149. A board about 4 in.
wide and from 12 in. to 18 in. long is fixed to the
bench or table with a bent screw. In the board is
a hole not quite so large as the diameter of the ball,
which is kept in place partly under and partly
within the hole by foot pressure exerted on a strap
or string passing over the outer end of the board as
illustrated. To alter the position of the ball, the
foot pressure is released. The above instructions
will be of help also in repairing cricket balls whose
seams have come undone.

The leather for a suit case should be such as
is used for straps of portmanteaus, etc. ; it is
smooth-grained and polished, and is made from
stout sides, small butts, etc. Cowhide can be
used, but will want a better backing.

When making the suit case, first cut a pattern
of stiff paper to the dimensions given below. Then
a case 6 in. high will need only 2 ft. of stitching,
while if the pattern were cut in separate pieces
there would be 13 ft. of stitching and less strength.
Fig. 150 shows the bottom, the centre of which
must measure within the dotted lines 20 in. by
13 in. Each of the four side-pieces A, B, C, and D
is 4 in. wide from the dotted line. The pattern
(Fig. 151) for the lid can be cut in the same way,
but the four pieces E, F, G, and H must be only
2 in. wide. Or the top and bottom sides may
measure $4\frac{1}{2}$ in. and $1\frac{1}{2}$ in. respectively, or the

bottom 6 in. and the lid (say) 1½ in., if the lid is to overlap the case; in such an instance the centre of the lid will need to be larger, in proportion to the substance of the material and its backing, but the first system is best and neatest.

For the backing and lining, patterns are cut for the two centres, and one of the sides (Fig. 150) is used as pattern for the four sides. Cut off one side (again to the dotted line) for the four sides of the lid. This will be better if done after the case is sewn. The pieces must be well fitted for each side and top and bottom, and they will want cover-

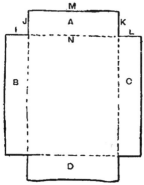

Fig. 150.—Bottom Piece of Suit Case.

ing with the lining, such as thin leather, drill, or sateen.

Mark across the two pieces of leather at the back just the same as the dotted lines in Figs. 150 and 151, and on these eight lines with a very small gouge a small groove must be made about half-way through the material. When cowhide is used a heavy mark will be sufficient, if one part is turned over flat on the other and gently tapped down on the right side.

To form true right-angles at the corners, squares should be cut out, as at I J and K L (Fig. 150), at both ends of the bottom piece.

The sewing can be done with about six or seven
strands of yellow flax, made into a thread as for
shoe-making; or the thread may be made in the
same way, and a harness-maker's needle used with
a diamond awl, each seam finishing firm and well
at the top and bottom.

Then fit the ten pieces of backing, which may
be pasteboard or stout cardboard, but thin leather-
board or wood pulpboard would be lightest. Cut
a small angular piece off all sides, or round up the
edges with fine sandpaper, covering one side of
each piece with lining material and leaving a

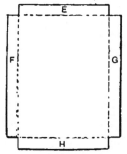

Fig. 151.—Lid of Suit Case.

margin all round to turn over to the other side.
This can be done to all four sides of the top and
bottom pieces, and the three sides of the four end-
pieces, as A, D, E, and H. Thus J, M, K (Fig. 150)
would have three smooth sides, while the bottom
part at N would hang loose with the four long
sides B, C, F, and G. Only the top of each need
be turned over, and these four sides can be glued
in first by applying a coat to the back and on the
rough ends of the lining that hang over. As each
is fixed (bookbinder's paste will do), glue the side
to which it is to be stuck, and fit it so that the
rough edge of the linen sticks on each end and
at the bottom. Putting in B first, then C, it will
be seen that each seam has a piece of this lining

to strengthen it and help to keep the case square.
Also when A and D are glued in, all four corners
are neat, and additional strength is also given all
round the edge of the bottom. The bottom can
now be stuck in, but in applying the glue, take
care not to bring it quite to the edge, stopping,
say, within ⅛ in. at least, or while fixing it in the
sides will be smeared.

A 46-in. strip of firm leather, 1½ in. wide, of the
material used for the outside can be either covered with thin brown Persian or left as it is. In
the latter case it will be well to sandpaper and
finish off the edge with a little brown cream. This
piece forms a sort of flange all round the front
and two ends, letting ½ in. be, as it were, inside
the bottom of the case, and 1 in. projecting above,

Fig. 152.—Section of Suit Case Side.

as shown by Q (Fig. 152), O being the bottom of
the case and P the side. This keeps the lid firmly
in its place, and prevents any wet getting in while
the case is carried. It can be stitched all round
to the top edge of the case, as shown at R. If
the lid is made to overlap, this piece is dispensed
with, and either the top can be stitched as a finish
or a copper rivet may be put through here and
there.

The handle can be made by cutting two pieces
of leather to shape and skiving them at the edge
to about half their thickness, and then stitching
the two together. If it is wanted thicker in the
middle, paste a long oval piece down the centre
before putting the two flesh sides together. This
can be secured on the front of the bottom of the
case by two copper rivets, or, better still, buy,

or make from a piece of strip brass, two square sockets for the handle. Each must be secured to the case by two small copper rivets, and each before fastening must have the handle put under, so that it crosses the handle. This will then have some play, and will lie flat while not in use, and lift sufficiently for the hand to go under; or one handle can be put at each end.

To finish the box, cut a strip of leather 2 in. wide and 1 ft. 8 in. long, put the lid on the case, and put the strip along the back, so that 1 in. of the width lies on the lid and the other inch on the case. Mark it right along on each side, take the lid off, and secure the piece to it by a row of small copper rivets or a row of stitching, and then repeat for fastening to the case.

A lock is easily added by cutting a portion of the front of the case away, inserting the lock, and riveting it on. Then close the case, fitting the hasp portion of the lock in position and riveting it in its place.

INDEX.

Made in the USA
Middletown, DE
22 February 2021

34170352R00099